NCIDQ FUNDAMENTALS
PRACTICE QUESTIONS AND MOCK EXAM

THIRD EDITION

DAVID KENT BALLAST, FAIA
NCIDQ CERTIFICATE NO. 9425

PPI®

PPI2PASS.COM
A **KAPLAN** COMPANY

Report Errors for This Book

PPI is grateful to every reader who notifies us of a possible error. Your feedback allows us to improve the quality and accuracy of our products. Report errata at **ppi2pass.com/errata**.

NCIDQ® is a registered trademark of the Council for Interior Design Qualification.

PPI is not affiliated with the Council for Interior Design Qualification (CIDQ®). PPI does not administer the NCIDQ Exam. PPI does not claim any endorsement or recommendation of its products or services by CIDQ.

MasterFormat® and SectionFormat® are registered trademarks of the Construction Specifications Institute.

LEED® is a registered trademark of the U.S. Green Building Council.

GreenSpec® is a registered trademark of Building Green, Inc.

NCIDQ Fundamentals Practice Questions and Mock Exam
Third Edition

Current release of this edition: 2

Release History

date	edition number	revision number	description
Jul 2021	3	1	New edition.
Aug 2022	3	2	Minor corrections.

PPI
ppi2pass.com

ISBN: 978-1-59126-843-7

TABLE OF CONTENTS

PREFACE AND ACKNOWLEDGMENTS

Every five years, the Council for Interior Design Qualification (CIDQ)[1] commissions a practice analysis to ensure the exam continues to accurately assess the knowledge and skills interior designers need to practice responsibly and to protect the health, safety, and welfare of the public. Results of the practice analysis are reported in the council's publication *Analysis of the Interior Design Profession*. The council administers three exams (the Interior Design Fundamentals Exam (IDFX), the Interior Design Professional Exam (IDPX), and the Interior Design Practicum (PRAC 2)) that cover the content areas identified in the analysis as being the essential tasks, knowledge, and skills of interior designers in the United States and Canada. I wrote *NCIDQ Fundamentals Practice Questions and Mock Exam* to be consistent with IDFX's content areas so that you will use it to prepare for and pass the IDFX.

In this third edition, I have reorganized questions and added new questions to be consistent with the 2021 NCIDQ exam content areas for the IDFX. Also included are new item types that the NCIDQ exam may use, including check-all-that-apply, fill-in-the-blank, hot spot, and drag-and-place. You will also find more questions based on illustrations.

I would like to thank Holly Williams Leppo, AIA, NCIDQ Certificate No. 19182, who reviewed the problems for validity and offered many good suggestions for additions and improvements. Many people have helped in the production of this book. I would like to thank Megan Synnestvedt, product director, Nicole Evans, senior product manager, Meghan Finley, content specialist, Beth Christmas, project manager, Tyler Hayes, editor, Bilal Baqai, editor, Scott Marley, editorial manager, Sean Woznicki, production editor, Richard Iriye, typesetter, Tom Bergstrom, production specialist, Kim Burton-Weisman, proofreader, Nikki Capra-McCaffrey, production manager, Sam Webster, publishing systems manager, and Grace Wong, director of editorial operations.

While I had a lot of help with this book, any mistakes are mine alone. If you find a mistake, please submit it through PPI's errata page at **ppi2pass.com/errata**. A reply will be posted and the error revised accordingly.

David Kent Ballast, FAIA
NCIDQ® Certificate No. 9425

---

[1]In this Preface, the Council for Interior Design Qualification is referred to as "the council," and the National Council for Interior Design Qualification exam as "the exam."

INTRODUCTION

HOW TO USE THIS BOOK

NCIDQ Fundamentals Practice Questions and Mock Exam was developed in accordance with the Council for Interior Design Qualification (CIDQ[1]) Interior Design Fundamentals Exam (IDFX) content areas. Though the exact questions in this book won't be found on the actual exam, they are like IDFX questions in terms of their format, level of difficulty, and the content areas they cover.

This book is dual-purpose and has two parts: 100 realistic practice questions and a 125-question mock exam. Both the practice questions and the mock exam are divided by content area to make it easy to focus your studying on content areas you are less familiar with.

Use the practice questions in the first part of this book to become familiar with the exam's content areas. Answers to the practice questions are given directly after the questions so you can immediately check your comprehension of a subject. Use the *NCIDQ Interior Design Reference Manual* (IDRM, also published by PPI) to research less familiar topics or questions answered incorrectly. Taking the time to research less familiar topics and incorrect answers will help you strengthen your understanding and ensure exam readiness.

Once you are comfortable with IDFX's content areas, use the mock exam in the second part of this book to simulate the exam experience. Put away study materials and references, set a timer for three hours, and answer as many of the mock exam questions as you can within the time limit. Complete the entire mock exam, trying to answer each question in no more than about 1 minute 15 seconds. If a question is likely to take longer, skip it. Note unanswered questions to go back to later and answer. This should leave a reserve of at least 20 minutes at the end of the exam session to review and at least guess at questions you left unanswered. Reread the questions you were able to answer only if there is extra time after guessing at all questions you marked to revisit. Be sure to mark an answer for every question. On IDFX,

---

[1]The Council for Interior Design Qualification is referred to as "the council" throughout this Introduction, while the National Council for Interior Design Qualification exam is referred to as "the exam."

unanswered questions are counted as wrong, so when you are unsure of an answer, make an educated guess among the most likely options.

If time runs out before you are able to complete all practice exam questions, make a note of the last question you answered within the time limit, but continue on to complete the entire practice exam. Keep track of time to determine how much faster you would need to work to finish the actual exam within three hours.

After completing the practice exam, check your selected answer options against the answer key. Each correct question is worth one point. There is no penalty for questions answered incorrectly. To score the practice exam, multiply the number of correct questions by 6.4.[2] A score of 500 or greater on the practice exam in this book is a passing score.

Use the fully explained answers at the end of the practice exam as a learning tool. Take note of the content areas with the most questions answered incorrectly, and focus the majority of your exam review around those.

ABOUT THE NCIDQ EXAM

The exam is divided into three sections: the Interior Design Fundamentals Exam (IDFX), the Interior Design Professional Exam (IDPX), and the Interior Design Practicum (PRAC). All three exams are administered via computer. IDFX contains questions that test the knowledge gained in school (e.g., programming and site analysis; design application and human behavior; design communication; life safety and universal design; interior building materials and finishes; technical specifications for furniture, fixtures, and equipment and lighting; construction document standards; and professional development and ethics). IDPX contains questions that test knowledge gained through work experience (e.g., project assessment and sustainability; project process, roles, and coordination; professional business practices; code requirements, laws, standards, and regulations; building systems and construction; integration of furniture, fixtures, and equipment; and contract administration). The Practicum contains exercises that test practical interior design knowledge (e.g., programming, planning, and analysis; code requirements, laws, standards, and regulations; integration with building systems; and contract documents). There is some content area overlap between the three exams. See "Eligibility" later in this Introduction for information on the requirements for each exam. All three exams are administered in April and October. Through Prometric, you can schedule your exams for any dates within those two months.

IDFX is three hours long with 125 questions (100 of which are scored). The remaining 25 questions are used for developmental purposes and are not scored. (These questions are not identified in advance.) Both IDFX and IDPX are scored on a scale of 200 to 800 points, with 500 being the minimum number of points needed to pass. Points are not deducted for questions answered incorrectly.

Exam Problem Types
There are several types of problems on IDFX, IDPX, and in this book

- multiple-choice problems
- check-all-that-apply problems

---

[2]On the actual exam, the council includes 25 unscored, experimental questions. To score the practice exam to parallel a real exam score, randomly choose 25 questions to leave unscored. Among the remaining 100 questions, calculate the number of correct questions and multiply this number by 8.0.

- fill-in-the-blank problems
- hot spot problems
- drag-and-place problems

Multiple-Choice Problems

Multiple-choice problems have two types. One type of multiple-choice problem is based on written, graphic, or photographic information. You will need to examine the information and select the correct answer from four given options. Some problems may require calculations. A second type of multiple-choice problem describes a situation that could be encountered in actual practice. Drawings, diagrams, photographs, forms, tables, or other data may also be given. The problem requires you to select the best answer from four options.

Multiple-choice problems often require you to do more than just select an answer based on memory. At times it will be necessary to combine several facts, analyze data, perform a calculation, or review a drawing.

Check-All-That-Apply Problems

Check-all-that-apply problems are a variation of a multiple-choice problem, where six options are given, and you must choose all the correct options. The problem tells how many of the options are correct, from two to four. You must choose all the correct options to receive credit; partial credit is not given.

Fill-in-the-Blank Problems

Fill-in-the-blank problems require you to fill in a blank with a value that you have derived from a table or a calculation.

Hot Spot Problems

Hot spot problems are used to assess visual judgment, evaluation, or prediction. Hot spot problems include the information needed to make a determination, along with an image (e.g., diagram, floor plan) and instructions on how to interact with the image. The problems will indicate that you should place a single target, also known as a hot spot icon, on the base image in the correct location or general area. On the exam, you will place the target on the image by moving the computer cursor to the correct location on the image and clicking on it. You will see crosshairs to help you position the point of click. You will be able to click on an alternate spot if you think your first choice is not correct. Your choice is not registered until you exit the problem. You can click anywhere within an acceptable area range and still be scored as correct.

Drag-and-Place Problems

Drag-and-place problems are similar to hot spot problems, but whereas hot spot problems involve placing just one target on the base image, drag-and-place problems involve placing two to six design elements or text onto the base image. Drag-and-place problems are used to assess visual judgment or evaluation with multiple pieces of information. The problem statement describes what information is to be used to make the determination, and provides instructions on how to interact with the image or graphic item.

A drag-and-place problem, for example, may require you to drag and place design elements such as wallboard trim onto the base image. On the exam, you will use the computer cursor to place the elements on the image by clicking and holding elements and dragging and releasing the elements on the correct location on the image. Depending on the question, you may use an element more than once or not at all. This type of question also provides an acceptable area range for placing the elements. The range may be small for questions about a detail or large for something like a floor plan.

Both IDFX and IDPX are machine-graded.

For more information and tips on how to prepare for IDFX, consult the *Interior Design Reference Manual* or visit PPI's website, **ppi2pass.com** (keywords: NCIDQ, IDRM).

The Practicum includes individual exercises that will require you to interpret a program, translate it into schematics, produce plan drawings, and develop appropriate specifications and schedules. Each exercise is scored by two NCIDQ graders. Graders give each exercise a score of 0, 1, 2, 4, or 5. There is no score of 3. Scores of 0, 1, and 2 are failing, and 4 and 5 are passing. If the exercise receives one passing and one failing score, a third NCIDQ grader will review the exercise. The two scores for each exercise are added together and multiplied by a weighting factor. The resulting value becomes a percentage of the raw score.

IDFX is three hours long with 125 questions (100 of which are scored), and IDPX is four hours long with 175 questions (150 of which are scored). The remaining 25 questions in each are used for developmental purposes and are not scored. (These questions are not identified in advance.) The Practicum is four hours long and includes 120 questions divided across three case studies.

IDFX Content Areas

The council uses its *Analysis of the Interior Design Profession* to develop the exam content areas, which cover the knowledge and skills that interior designers must possess to protect public health, safety, and welfare. For IDFX and IDPX, the number of questions in each content area is related to that content area's relative importance, as evaluated through survey responses from practicing interior designers.

The content areas for IDFX are as follows. The percentage of weight for each content area is given in parentheses.

Interior Design Fundamentals Exam (IDFX)

I. Programming and Site Analysis (10%)

Demonstrate appropriate use of

- analysis tools (e.g., spreadsheets, site photographs, matrices, bubble diagrams, graphs, behavioral-based analytics)

Demonstrate understanding of

- research methods (e.g., observations, interviewing, surveying, case studies, benchmarking, precedent studies)
- the site context (e.g., location, views, solar orientation, zoning, historical information, constraints, change of use, transportation)

II. Relationship Between Human Behavior and the Designed Environment (10%)

Demonstrate understanding of

- human factors (e.g., ergonomics, anthropometrics, proxemics, psychological, physiological, social)
- universal design (e.g., accessibility, ability level, inclusivity, special needs, aging population, bariatric, pediatric)

- contextual influences (e.g., environmental and ecological, social, cultural, aesthetic, hierarchy of needs)

Demonstrate knowledge of

- sensory considerations (e.g., acoustics, lighting, visual stimuli, color response, scent, tactile, thermal comfort)

III. Design Communication Techniques (10%)

Ability to apply

- data and research (e.g., charts, infographics, analytics)
- conceptual diagrams (e.g., parti diagrams, bubble diagrams, adjacency matrices)
- planning diagrams (e.g., stacking/zoning diagrams, block plans/square footage allocations)

IV. Life Safety and Universal Design (20%)

Demonstrate understanding of

- life safety (e.g., egress, fire separation, fire-rated partitions and doors, and A/V alarms location coordination)
- universal design (e.g., inclusive design, accessible design)

V. Interior Building Materials and Finishes (10%)

Demonstrate understanding of

- textiles (e.g., types, testing standards and codes, applications, installation methods, estimating, technical specifications)
- floor coverings (e.g., types, transitions, testing standards and codes, applications, installation methods, estimating, slip resistance, technical specifications)
- wall treatments (e.g., types, testing standards and codes, applications, installation methods, estimating, technical specifications)
- window treatments (e.g., types, testing standards and codes, applications, installation methods, estimating, technical specifications)
- ceiling treatments (e.g., types, testing standards and codes, applications, installation methods, estimating, technical specifications)
- acoustical products (e.g., types, testing standards and codes, applications, installation methods, estimating, technical specifications)
- wayfinding and signage (e.g., types, testing standards and codes, applications, installation methods, estimating, technical specifications)

VI. Technical Specifications for Furniture, Fixtures, & Equipment and Lighting (15%)

Demonstrate understanding of

- life safety elements (e.g., flammability, toxicity, slip resistance, accessibility and egress clearances, fixed and loose furniture, indoor air quality, code compliance)
- sustainability and environmental impact (e.g., recyclability, cradle to cradle, embodied energy, carbon footprint, material sourcing, ratings and certifications)
- materials and technical specifications (e.g., color fastness, abrasion resistance, cleanability, reference standards, ANSI/BIFMA)

- light fixture selection and specification (e.g., general, accent and task lighting; color temperature, color rendering, lamp types, energy load)

VII.   Construction Drawings, Schedules, and Specifications (20%)

Demonstrate understanding of

- code required information (e.g., egress, accessibility, specialty codes, fire/life safety, occupancy, plumbing calculations)
- appropriate measuring conventions (e.g., scale, unit of measure, dimensioning)
- construction drawing standards (e.g., annotations, hatch patterns, line types, symbols, north arrow, section cuts, cross referencing)

Understand and develop

- general information sheets (e.g., general conditions and notes, drawing index, legend, symbols, location, consultant, contact information)
- demolition plans
- floor plans (e.g., partition plan, construction plan, dimension plan)
- reflected ceiling and/or lighting plans (e.g., supplies, returns, ceiling types, heights, monitoring and detection devices, switching, controls)
- furniture plans
- finish plans
- elevations, sections, and details (e.g., partition types, enlarged plans, custom details and assemblies)
- power, data, and communication plans
- schedules (e.g., finish, equipment, plumbing, lighting, door, window, hardware, accessories)
- millwork (e.g., construction techniques, coordination with furniture, fixtures, and equipment, and utilities, substrates, shop drawings, material selection, accessibility)

VIII.   Professional Development and Ethics (5%)

Demonstrate understanding of

- professional ethics (e.g., code of ethics, consumer protection, health, safety, welfare, social responsibility)
- professional development (e.g., professional organizations, continuing education)

HOW TO REGISTER FOR THE EXAM

Registering for the exam is a multi-step process. First, you must meet the exam's eligibility requirements, then submit an application and have it accepted. Confirm your eligibility, and begin the application process well before the exam date.

Eligibility

You may take IDFX after you have met the minimum education requirements. You may meet the education requirements by receiving a bachelor of arts or master of fine arts degree from an interior design program accredited by the Council for Interior Design Accreditation (CIDA); a bachelor of arts degree or higher from an interior design program *not* accredited by CIDA with at least 60 semester (or 90 quarter) credits in interior design coursework; a bachelor of arts degree or higher in another major with at least 60 semester (or 90 quarter) credits of interior design coursework that led to a diploma, degree, or certificate; an associate of arts degree with at least 40 semester (or 60 quarter) units in interior design; or a bachelor of arts or master of fine arts degree from an architecture program accredited by the National Architectural Accrediting Board (NAAB) or Canadian Architectural Certification Board (CACB).

You may take IDPX and the Practicum after you have met the education and work experience requirements given in this section. Work experience for which academic credit was received will not count toward the hours required. Passing IDFX is not a prerequisite to taking IDPX and the Practicum, although you must receive a passing score on all three exam sections to earn the NCIDQ certificate.

To be eligible for IDPX and the Practicum with a bachelor of arts or master of fine arts degree from an interior design program accredited by CIDA, you must complete 3520 hours of work experience.[3] At least 1760 of those hours must be accrued after you have met your education requirements.

To be eligible for IDPX and the Practicum with a bachelor of arts degree or higher from an interior design program that is *not* accredited by CIDA, you must complete 3520 hours of work experience. At least 1760 of those hours must be accrued after you have met your education requirements. In addition, at least 60 semester (or 90 quarter) credits must be in interior design coursework.

To be eligible for IDPX and the Practicum with a bachelor of arts degree or higher in another major, you must complete 3520 hours of work experience. At least 1760 of those hours must be accrued after you have met your education requirements. In addition, at least 60 semester (or 90 quarter) credits of interior design coursework must be completed and must have resulted in a diploma, degree, or certificate.

To be eligible for IDPX and the Practicum with an associate of arts degree of 60 semester (or 90 quarter) units in interior design, you must complete 5280 hours of work experience. All these hours must be accrued after you have met your education requirements.

To be eligible for IDPX and the Practicum with an associate of arts degree of 40 semester (or 60 quarter) units in interior design, you must complete 7040 hours of work experience. All these hours must be accrued after you have met your education requirements.

To be eligible for IDPX and the Practicum with a bachelor of arts or master of fine arts degree from an architecture program accredited by NAAB or CACB, you must complete 5280 hours of work experience. All these hours must be accrued after you have met your education requirements.

Applying

Exam dates and application deadlines are listed on PPI's website at **ppi2pass.com** (keyword: NCIDQ). The first step in the application process is submitting the online

---

[3]Hours worked under an NCIDQ certificate holder, a licensed/registered interior designer, or an architect who offers interior design services count as "qualified" work experience, and accrue at 100%. Hours worked in alternative situations accrue at lower rates. Hours worked under direct supervision by an interior designer who is not registered, licensed, or an NCIDQ certificate holder accrue at a rate of 75%; work sponsored, but not directly supervised, by the same individual accrues at a rate of 25%. Work hours not supervised by a designer (i.e., supervised by someone other than a designer, or not supervised at all in the case of self-employment) accrue at a rate of 25%. The Interior Design Experience Program (IDEP) offered by the council satisfies the work experience requirement.

application form and application fee through MyNCIDQ, a section of CIDQ's website (cidq.org). For IDFX, gather the following supporting materials and apply online through MyNCIDQ. Unopened official transcripts should be mailed.

- *Official transcripts:* Download the transcript request form from the council's website and submit it to the registrar (along with any fees the registrar requires) for each college or university you attended. The registrar will return the official transcript to you in a sealed envelope which must be included, *unopened*, in your package of supporting materials.

For IDPX and the Practicum, the following items are also needed.

- *Work experience verification forms:* Submit a separate form for each position you held. Complete the direct supervision work experience verification form for work experience you completed under a direct supervisor. For work experience not directly supervised by a design professional (for example, in the case of self-employment), complete the sponsored work experience verification form. A sponsor is a design professional who can verify work experience, but was not a direct supervisor and may not have had direct control over or detailed knowledge of your work.

Do not include any additional materials in your package of supporting materials. Any additional documents you include will be discarded. Be sure to have all materials submitted by the relevant deadline; the council will not review a partial application or an application once the deadline has passed.

Registering

If your application is accepted by the council, you will be notified through MyNCIDQ. If your application is not accepted, you may need further education and work experience to fulfill the requirements. If this process takes more than one year, you will need to resubmit your entire application.

If your application is accepted, you may register for as many exam sections as you were accepted for. If you choose not to register for this exam cycle, you will remain an active candidate and will receive email notifications about registering for the next exam cycle. Fees are listed in the registration guide (a brochure available for download from the council's website) for each exam section.

Registering Through Prometric

To register for IDFX or IDPX, go to Prometric's website (**prometric.com**). Choose the exam location and date from those available. All locations accept registrations up to a day before the exam; some locations accept same-day registration. Registration fees are payable by credit card only.

Prometric will send you an email with your registration confirmation and test center information. Bring two forms of identification with you on examination day. One of these must be a government-issued photo ID.

Registering Through MyNCIDQ

To register for the Practicum, to MyNCIDQ and click on "Exam Registration." Complete the confidentiality agreement and statement of responsibility. Registration fees are payable online by credit card.

The council will send you an email with further exam information after receipt of payment and an email with your letter of admission at least two weeks prior to the exam. Print the letter of admission and present it with a government-issued photo ID on examination day.

IDFX TIPS

Consider the following tips for taking IDFX.

- Try to complete each question in no more than 1 minute 15 seconds to leave a reserve of about 20 minutes to guess at unanswered questions at the end of the exam session.

- Eliminate any obviously incorrect options before attempting to guess. The chances of guessing correctly are better between two choices than among four.

- Look for an exception to a rule or a special circumstance that makes the obvious, easy response incorrect. Although there may be a few easy and obvious questions, it's more likely that a simple question has a level of complexity that is not immediately obvious.

- Take note of absolute words such as "always," "never," or "completely." These words often indicate some minor exception that can turn what reads like a true statement into a false statement, or vice versa.

- Watch for words like "seldom," "usually," "best," or "most reasonable." These words generally indicate that some judgment will be involved in answering the question, so look for two or more options that may be very similar.

- If a question appears to be fundamentally flawed, make the best choice possible under the circumstances. Flawed questions do not appear often on the exam, but when they do, they are usually discovered by the council in the grading process. These questions will not negatively impact your score.

WHAT TO DO AFTER THE EXAM

Score notifications for IDFX and IDPX will be sent within eight weeks after your test date. Score notifications for the Practicum will be sent within 14 weeks after your test date. If you pass the Practicum, you will receive a score report that indicates "Pass." If you fail the Practicum, you will receive a score report that indicates "Fail," along with a list of the exercises receiving failing scores. If you fail one or two of the three exam sections, you will only need to retake the failed section(s). Your state or province may impose restrictions on the number of years you can wait between taking different sections of the exam.

The council will issue you a certificate and a certificate number when you pass all three exam sections. The certificate number will be unique, and is used to distinguish designers within the interior design field. To identify yourself as an NCIDQ certificate holder on stationery, business cards, and so on, use the following format: "[First name] [Last name], NCIDQ® Certificate No. [######]." For example, "David Ballast, NCIDQ® Certificate No. 9425."

To maintain active status as an NCIDQ certificate holder, you must pay a yearly certificate renewal fee. You will receive your first renewal notice one year after your exam date.

HOW SI UNITS ARE USED IN THIS BOOK

This book uses customary U.S. units (also called English or inch-pound units) as the primary measuring system and includes equivalent measurements in the text and illustrations, using the Système International d'Unités (SI), commonly called the metric system. The use of SI units for construction and publishing in the United States is problematic because the building construction industry (with the exception of federal construction) has generally not adopted metric units. Equivalent measurements of customary U.S. units are usually given as *soft* conversions, whereas customary U.S. measurements are simply converted into SI units using standard conversion factors. Standard conversion results in a number with excessive significant digits. When construction is done using SI units, the building is designed and drawn according to *hard* conversions (defined by industry convention, not math), where planning dimensions and building products are based on a metric module from the beginning. For example, studs are spaced 400 mm on center to accommodate panel products that are manufactured in standard 1200 mm widths.

As the United States transitions to using SI units, code-writing bodies, federal laws (such as the Americans with Disabilities Act, or ADA), product manufacturers, trade associations, and other construction-related industries typically still use the customary U.S. system and make soft conversions to develop SI equivalents. Some manufacturers produce the same product using both measuring systems. Although there are industry standards for developing SI equivalents, there is no consistent method used for rounding off conversions. For example, the *International Building Code* (IBC) shows a 152 mm equivalent when a 6 in dimension is required. The *Americans with Disabilities Act and Architectural Barriers Act Accessibility Guidelines* (*ADA/ABA Guidelines*) gives a 150 mm equivalent for the same customary U.S. dimension.

To further complicate matters, each publisher may employ a slightly different house style in handling SI equivalents when customary U.S. units are used as the primary measuring system. The confusion is likely to continue until the United States construction industry adopts the SI system completely, precluding the need for dual dimensioning in publishing.

For the purposes of this book, the following conventions have been adopted.

- When dimensions are for informational use, the SI equivalent rounded to the nearest millimeter is used.

- When dimensions relate to planning or design guidelines, the SI equivalent is rounded to the nearest 5 mm for numbers over a few inches and to the nearest 10 mm for numbers over a few feet. When the dimension exceeds several feet, the number is rounded to the nearest 100 mm. For example, if a given activity requires a space about 10 ft wide, the modular, rounded SI equivalent will be given as 3000 mm. More exact conversions are not required.

- When an item is manufactured only to a customary U.S. measurement, the nearest SI equivalent rounded to the nearest millimeter is given, unless the dimension is very small (as for metal gages), in which case a more precise decimal equivalent will be given. Some materials, such as glass, are often manufactured to SI sizes. For example, a nominal $^1/_2$ in thick piece of glass will have an SI equivalent of 13 mm but can be ordered as 12 mm.

- When there is a hard conversion in the industry and an SI equivalent item is manufactured, the hard conversion is given. For example, a 24 in × 24 in ceiling tile would have the hard conversion of 600 mm × 600 mm (instead of 610 mm) because this size is manufactured and available in the United States.

- When an SI conversion is used by a code, such as the IBC, or published in another regulation, such as the *ADA/ABA Guidelines*, the SI equivalents used by the issuing agency are printed in this book. For example, the same 10 ft dimension given previously as 3000 mm for a planning guideline would have a building code SI equivalent of 3048 mm because this is what the IBC requires. The *ADA/ABA Guidelines* generally follow the rounding rule of taking SI dimensions to the nearest 10 mm. For example, a 10 ft requirement for accessibility will be shown as 3050 mm. The code requirements for readers outside the United States may be slightly different.

- Throughout this book, the customary U.S. measurements are given first, and the SI equivalents follow in parentheses. In text, SI units are always given. For example, a dimension might be indicated as 4 ft 8 in (1420 mm). In illustrations, however, standard convention is followed; the SI equivalent is usually without units and is assumed to be in millimeters unless other units are given. The same measurement in an illustration would appear as 4′ 8″ (1420).

PPI, a Kaplan Company • ppi2pass.com

CODES, STANDARDS, AND REFERENCES FOR THE EXAM

CODES AND STANDARDS

IDFX covers information related to the following codes and standards.

ADA/ABA Guidelines: Americans with Disabilities Act and Architectural Barriers Act Accessibility Guidelines. U.S. Access Board, Washington, DC. www.wbdg.org/ffc/usab/guidelines-standards/ada-aba-guidelines-standards.

BOMA: *BOMA Office Standards Z65.1*, 2017. Building Owners and Managers Association International, Washington, DC.

IBC: *International Building Code*, 2018. International Code Council, Washington, DC.

ICC: *A117.1 Accessible and Usable Buildings and Facilities*, 2009. International Code Council, Washington, DC.

IPC: *International Plumbing Code*, 2018. International Code Council, Washington, DC.

NFPA: *NFPA 101 Life Safety Code*, 2021. National Fire Protection Association, Quincy, MA.

REFERENCES

The following references contain information about the interior design field, including information specific to IDFX content areas. These references may be useful to review as you prepare for the exam.

Allison, Diana. *Estimating and Costing for Interior Designers*. Bloomsbury/Fairchild Books.

Ballast, David Kent. *Interior Construction and Detailing for Designers and Architects*. PPI.

Ballast, David Kent. *Interior Design Reference Manual: Everything You Need to Know to Pass the NCIDQ Exam*. PPI.

Binggeli, Corky. *Building Systems for Interior Designers*. Hoboken, NJ: John Wiley and Sons.

Birren, Faber. *Color and Human Response*. Hoboken, NJ: John Wiley and Sons.

Botti-Salitsky, Rose Mary. *Programming and Research: Skills and Techniques for Interior Designers, second edition*. Bloomsbury.

Brooker, Graeme & Weinthal, Lois. *The Handbook of Interior Architecture and Design*. Bloomsbury.

Bush, Pamela McCauley. *Ergonomics: Foundational Principles, Applications, and Technologies*. CRC Press.

Ching, Francis D. K. *Architecture: Form, Space, and Order*. Hoboken, NJ: John Wiley and Sons.

Ching, Francis D. K., and Corky Binggeli. *Interior Design Illustrated*. Hoboken, NJ: John Wiley and Sons.

Coleman, Cindy. *Interior Design Handbook of Professional Practice*. New York, NY: McGraw-Hill Professional Publishing.

Deasy, C. M. *Designing Places for People: A Handbook on Human Behavior for Architects, Designers, and Facility Managers*. New York, NY: Whitney Library of Design.

Farren, Carol E. *Planning and Managing Interior Projects, second edition*. R.S. Means Company, Ins.

Godsey, Lisa. *Interior Design Materials and Specifications, third edition*. Bloomsbury/Fairchild Books.

Gordon, Gary. *Interior Lighting for Designers, fifth edition*. John Wiley & Sons, Inc.

Grandzik, Walter T., Alison G. Kwok, Benjamin Stein, and John S. Reynolds. *Mechanical and Electrical Equipment for Buildings*. Hoboken, NJ: John Wiley and Sons.

Granet, Keith. *The Business of Design: Balancing Creativity and Profitability*. Princeton Architectural Press (Chronical Books).

Hall, Edward T. *The Hidden Dimension*. New York, NY: Anchor Books.

Hall, Edward T. *The Silent Language*. New York, NY: Anchor Books.

Karlen, Mark. *Space Planning Basics*. Hoboken, NJ: John Wiley and Sons.

Kilmer, W. Otie and Rosemary Kilmer. *Construction Drawings and Details for Interiors: Basic Skills*. Hoboken, NJ: John Wiley and Sons.

Knackstedt, Mary V. *The Interior Design Business Handbook: A Complete Guide to Profitability, fifth edition*. John Wiley & Sons, Inc.

Koe, Frank Theodore. *Fabric for the Designed Interior, second edition*. Bloomsbury/Fairchild Books.

Koper, Dak. *Environmental Psychology for Design, second edition*. Fairchild Books.

Lechner, Norbert. *Heating, Cooling, Lighting: Sustainable Design Methods for Architects, fourth edition*. John Wiley & Sons, Inc.

Mahnke, Frank H. *Color, Environment, and Human Response*. Hoboken, NJ: John Wiley and Sons.

McGowan, Maryrose. *Specifying Interiors: A Guide to Construction and FE&E for Commercial Interiors Projects*. Hoboken, NJ: John Wiley and Sons.

McGowan, Maryrose, and Kelsey Kruse, eds. *Interior Graphic Standards.* Hoboken, NJ: John Wiley and Sons.

Mitton, Maureen. *Interior Design Visual Presentation: A Guide to Graphics, Models, and Presentation Techniques, fifth edition.* John Wiley & Sons, Inc.

Mitton, Maureen and Nystuen, Courtney. *Residential Interior Design: A Guide to Planning Spaces, third edition.* John Wiley & Sons, Inc.

Nussbaumer, Linda L. *Human Factors in the Built Environment, second edition.* Bloomsbury/ Fairchild Books.

Piotrowski, Christine M. *Professional Practice for Interior Designers.* Hoboken, NJ: John Wiley and Sons.

Reznikoff, S. C. *Interior Graphic and Design Standards.* New York, NY: Whitney Library of Design.

Reznikoff, S. C. *Specifications for Commercial Interiors: Professional Liabilities, Regulations, and Performance Criteria.* New York, NY: Whitney Library of Design.

Rhoads, Marcela Abadi. *Applying the ADA: Designing for the 2010 Americans with Disabilities Act – Standards for Accessible Design in Multiple Building Types.* John Wiley & Sons, Inc..

Slotkis, Susan J. *Foundations of Interior Design, third edition.* Fairchild Books.

Steinfeld, Edward and Maisel, Jordana L. *Universal Design: Creating Inclusive Environments.* John Wiley & Sons, Inc..

Tucker, Lisa M. *Designing Sustainable Residential and Commercial Interiors: Applying Concepts and Practices, first edition.* Fairchild Books.

Tucker, Lisa M. *International Building Codes and Guidelines for Interior Design.* Bloomsbury/ Fairchild Books.

Tucker, Lisa M. *Sustainable Building Systems and Construction for Designers, second edition.* Bloomsbury/Fairchild Books.

U.S. Green Building Council. *LEED Reference Guide for Green Interior Design and Construction.* Washington, DC: U.S. Green Building Council.

Wakita, Osamu A. and Linde, Richard M. *The Professional Practice of Architectural Working Drawings, fifth edition.* John Wiley & Sons, Inc.

Wilson, Travis Kelly. *Drafting and Design: Basics for Interior Design.* Fairchild Books.

Winchip, Susan M. *Fundamentals of Lighting, third edition.* Bloomsbury/Fairchild Books.

Winchip, Susan M. *Professional Practice for Interior Designers in the Global Marketplace.* Bloomsbury/Fairchild Books.

Winchip, Susan M. *Sustainable Design for Interior Environments, second edition.* Fairchild Books.

Yates, MaryPaul and Concra, Adrienne. *Textiles for Residential and Commercial Interiors, fifth edition.* Fairchild Books.

PRACTICE QUESTIONS

❶ PROGRAMMING AND SITE ANALYSIS

1. Which type of plan is always needed to begin space planning in an existing building?

(A) base plan

(B) circulation plan

(C) exiting plan

(D) reflected ceiling plan

The answer is A. A base plan shows the layout of the existing building. It is always needed to begin the interior design space plan.

2. For most planning problems, the MOST efficient type of circulation system is a

(A) radial system

(B) single-loaded corridor system

(C) double-loaded corridor system

(D) grid system

The answer is C. Because a double-loaded corridor system serves rooms on both sides of it in a straight line, this is the most efficient option for most interiors. Radial and grid systems generally have much higher proportions of corridor to space served than double-loaded systems do.

3. According to William Peña's book, *Problem Seeking*, all design problems can be stated in terms of form and which three other factors?

(A) analysis, synthesis, and function

(B) function, economy, and time

(C) goals, facts, and function

(D) economy, time, and synthesis

The answer is B. Design problems can be stated in terms of form, function, economy, and time. Each of these statements can be further broken down into more specific terms. For example, economy can be studied in terms of initial cost, operating cost, and life-cycle cost.

4. Interior spaces often need to be multifunctional or flexible. What are the three components of flexibility as a programmatic design concept?

    (A) versatility, convertibility, and grouping
    (B) expandability, hierarchy, and flow
    (C) flow, hierarchy, and convertibility
    (D) convertibility, expandability, and versatility

The answer is D. The three components of flexibility are convertibility, expandability, and versatility. *Convertibility* refers to a space's usefulness for different functions through the conversion of the space. *Expandability* refers to a space's ability to accommodate growth through expansion. *Versatility* refers to a space's ability to accommodate a variety of activities.

5. A residential design in a rural area involves the addition of two bedrooms and two bathrooms. Which of the following should be the two GREATEST concerns during the home's due diligence investigation?

    (A) neighborhood character and zoning setbacks
    (B) zoning setbacks and septic capacity
    (C) heating system capacity and septic capacity
    (D) zoning height limitations and heating system capacity

The answer is C. Rural areas tend to use septic tank systems rather than sewer systems. Because the addition includes two bathrooms, the home's septic capacity should be a primary concern during the due diligence investigation. The addition of two bedrooms would also increase the home's heating requirements, so the heating system's capacity should also be a primary concern of the investigation.

Although zoning setbacks, neighborhood character, and zoning heights should be reviewed in any due diligence investigation, they are less of a concern in rural areas than in cities because rural houses are typically much farther apart.

6. A new office suite is planned for the fifth floor of a building. Which of the following existing characteristics would MOST affect egress planning?

    (A) location of stairs and presence of a sprinkler system
    (B) size of the existing building and fire rating of the existing corridors
    (C) area and shape of the fifth floor and location of stairs
    (D) location of the elevators and area of the fifth floor

The answer is C. The location of the stairs is the primary factor in determining where and how the new space's exit access door or doors should be located. Exit access travel distance and the number and length of dead-end corridors should all be minimized, and the common path of egress travel should be considered. Furthermore, the area and shape of the existing floor plate could affect the exit access travel distance and, therefore, the layout of the new space.

The presence of a sprinkler system could have an effect on egress planning, but a smaller one. The fire rating of the existing corridors and the location of the elevators will generally have little or no effect on where to locate the exit access doors.

7. During preliminary planning for a day care center in a low-rise office building, the interior designer discovers that the zoning ordinance limits the area of such centers to about 20% less than the client's programmed needs. How could the interior designer best attempt to resolve the problem?

(A) apply for a conditional use permit

(B) suggest the client apply for a variance

(C) reduce the area planned to that allowed

(D) appeal to the local planning commission

The answer is B. A variance is a deviation from zoning regulations. The interior designer could assist the client in applying for a variance and present the case to the zoning board. In the case of a day care center requesting a relatively small size increase, it is likely that the hardship would be recognized and a variance granted.

A conditional use permit is typically used to allow a nonconforming use in a zoning district and would not be the appropriate way to solve the problem. It is unlikely that the client would want to decrease the size of the planned center. The local planning commission would not be involved with this kind of issue.

8. Preliminary space planning shows that it is impossible to satisfy all the programmed adjacencies shown on the adjacency matrix, which has been approved by the client. What is the BEST course of action?

(A) Verify that the adjacencies require physical connection, and then review the problem with the client.

(B) Satisfy as many adjacency connections as possible, and present this information to the client for review and approval.

(C) Ask the client to downgrade the importance of the problematic adjacencies.

(D) Develop several alternatives that come as close as possible to the requirements, and have the client select the one that best satisfies the program.

The answer is A. Option A lets the client clarify the programming adjacencies and, if necessary, modify them so the designer can proceed with good information. If the client wants to see sketches to prove that the required adjacencies cannot be made to work, these are already available from the initial work on the problem.

Options B and D are possible but require that the designer make guesses and do a lot of work before the client reviews the problem. Option C is risky because the problematic adjacencies may turn out to be the most important ones for the client, while the ones easily achieved may be less important.

9. An accurate representation of materials can BEST be shown with a

(A) computer rendering

(B) full-size mockup

(C) presentation model

(D) study model

The answer is B. A full-size mockup of an actual material would be the best way to represent the materials accurately.

10. An interior designer typically develops color and material boards during the

(A) design development phase only

(B) schematic design phase only

(C) programming and schematic design phases

(D) schematic design and design development phases

The answer is D. In most cases, the selection of finishes and furniture begins during the schematic design phase. The selection is then refined and finalized during the design development phase, before drawings and specifications are finalized in the construction document phase.

❷ RELATIONSHIP BETWEEN HUMAN BEHAVIOR AND THE DESIGNED ENVIRONMENT

11. Which of the following would be the MOST important consideration in the design of ergonomically correct chairs for air traffic controllers?

(A) adjustability

(B) firm cushions

(C) lumbar support

(D) tilt and swivel capability

The answer is A. All the options are important considerations in designing ergonomically correct chairs. However, at most airports air traffic control is in operation around the clock, so the same chair will be used by different people at different times, and each person will be sitting in the chair for long stretches. Because of this, it is most important that the chair be easily adjustable to accommodate variations in body size.

12. An interior designer would MOST likely use anthropometric information to

(A) design countertops for a public restroom

(B) determine the percentage of children who would be comfortable on custom-designed benches in a puppet theater

(C) develop the best position for multiple VDT screens in a stock trader's workstation

(D) evaluate a new chair design that has just come on the market

The answer is B. Anthropometrics is primarily concerned with measuring the size of the human body and developing dimensional ranges within which certain percentages of a given population fall. Such raw data would be directly useful for choosing the height, depth, and other aspects of the benches so that the greatest percentage of children would be comfortable seated on them. The other options relate more to ergonomics, or human interaction with the environment.

13. Thermal comfort for a person sitting in a classroom depends on

   (A) air temperature and humidity only
   (B) clothing type, air temperature, and air movement
   (C) air movement, convection, radiation, and conduction
   (D) air movement, air temperature, radiation, and humidity

The answer is D. These are the four basic components to human thermal comfort: air movement, air temperature, radiation, and humidity. Although air temperature and humidity are two of the most critical aspects of comfort, they alone are not sufficient to describe it. Clothing can moderate the effects of air temperature, but it is not one of the basic components of comfort. Conduction is a very minor part of how the human body gains and loses heat.

14. Which of the following should the interior designer cite to support the inclusion of a large expanse of glass in a new office design?

   (A) design theory
   (B) factual evidence
   (C) Gestalt psychology
   (D) programmatic concepts

The answer is B. The interior designer should cite factual evidence for this decision. The client is more likely to be persuaded by evidence of measurable benefits than by theories or philosophies. For example, studies conducted by the U.S. Department of Energy have found that natural light and visual access to the outside can increase the health, comfort, and productivity of building occupants.

The term for the design approach that uses quantitative and qualitative research to support design decisions is *evidence-based design*. Design theory directs designs based on personal philosophies or beliefs. Gestalt psychology holds that humans perceive things as larger wholes, not as individual bits of stimulus. Programmatic concepts are statements about functional solutions to a client's performance requirements.

15. Which seating group shown would be BEST for planning a waiting area to accommodate six people in a health clinic?

(A)

(B)

(C)

(D)

The answer is A. Because a waiting area is generally filled with strangers who prefer not to share the same sofa, a layout that provides individual seating is best, which eliminates options B and D. Option A is better than option C because it makes it easier for people to circulate to and from the chairs, and it increases the distance between people facing each other if all chairs are occupied.

16. Of the open-plan workstations shown, which is MOST efficient and well suited for frequent visitor conferences?

(A)

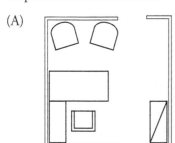

(B)

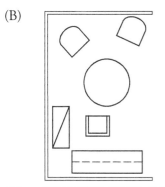

(C)

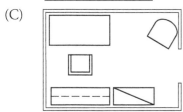

(D)

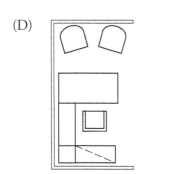

The answer is D. Layout D is the only one that is both efficient and appropriate for frequent visitor conferences. Layouts A and B are appropriate for frequent conferences, but neither uses space as efficiently as Layout D. Layout C is efficient but not well suited for frequent visitor conferences because it would be difficult for the worker to get to his or her desk when a visitor was present and because the arrangement of the chairs would make talking awkward.

17. On the drawing shown, place the recommended dimensions for comfortable seating at a residential dining table in the boxes given. Some dimensions may not be required.

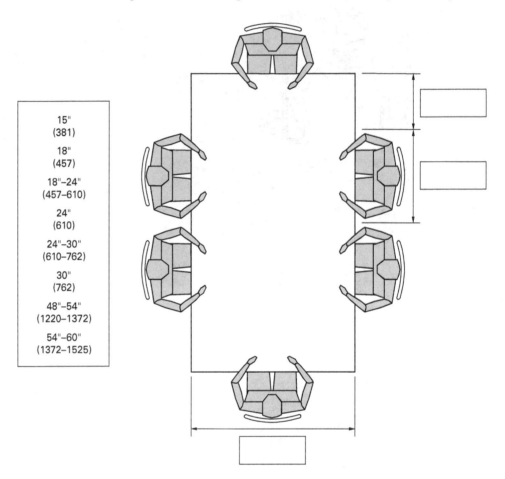

15"
(381)

18"
(457)

18"–24"
(457–610)

24"
(610)

24"–30"
(610–762)

30"
(762)

48"–54"
(1220–1372)

54"–60"
(1372–1525)

For comfortable dining, a 30 in (762 mm) width should be provided for each person, with an allowance of 18 in (457 mm) at the ends of the table for those diners. An 18 in (457 mm) depth should be allowed for each diner's place setting, with a 12 in to 18 in (305 mm to 457 mm) area in the center of the table. This gives a recommended table width of 48 in to 54 in (1220 mm to 1372 mm).

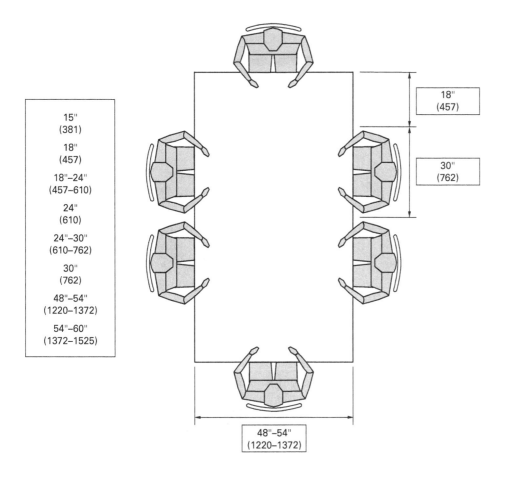

15"
(381)

18"
(457)

18"–24"
(457–610)

24"
(610)

24"–30"
(610–762)

30"
(762)

48"–54"
(1220–1372)

54"–60"
(1372–1525)

18"
(457)

30"
(762)

48"–54"
(1220–1372)

18. The given plan drawing diagrammatically illustrates a built-in seating arrangement within a larger room. Which Gestalt principle informs how the overall shape would be perceived?

(A) simplicity

(B) grouping

(C) continuity

(D) closure

The answer is D. In Gestalt psychology, closure is the human tendency to perceive an incomplete form as complete. This tendency is especially strong when the form suggests a simple shape such as a circle or square. The seating arrangement shown in the drawing strongly suggests a circle.

19. Which of the following design principles would MOST appropriately govern the design of a hotel lobby?

 (A) functionalism

 (B) proxemics

 (C) regionalism

 (D) symbolism

The answer is B. Hotel lobbies provide a variety of functions for occupants who generally do not know one another. Therefore, proxemics—which deals with the spacing between people and the organization of those spaces—would be the most important design principle in the design of a hotel lobby. Using proxemics, the interior designer could determine the lobby's ideal front desk layout, waiting area configuration, furniture types and positions, and overall size.

While the designer could also incorporate the principles of functionalism (e.g., simple, no extraneous decoration), regionalism (e.g., design reflecting local geographic area), and symbolism (e.g., using representative symbols) into the lobby decor, its overall design would best be governed by proxemics.

20. A designer uses the principle of harmony in order to

 (A) develop visual consistency and equilibrium among individual elements

 (B) elicit compositional unity from different elements

 (C) establish two elements as more important than the others in a composition

 (D) provide variation in the elements of a composition

The answer is B. Harmony is used to create a feeling of compositional unity from elements that are different from one another. Option A relates more to balance and repetition. Option C describes the principle of emphasis. Option D is incorrect because harmony is used to unify a composition rather than provide variation, even though variation is often part of a harmonious design.

❸ DESIGN COMMUNICATION TECHNIQUES

21. Adjacency requirements for the physical movement of goods in a manufacturing plant would BEST be illustrated with a(n)

 (A) adjacency matrix

 (B) bubble diagram

 (C) flowchart

 (D) stacking diagram

The answer is C. In a manufacturing plant, goods travel from one station to another during the process of fabrication. A flowchart would show the adjacencies as well as the steps in the process of manufacture. A bubble diagram would show the adjacencies but not necessarily the specific sequence of manufacture. Neither an adjacency matrix nor a stacking diagram would adequately illustrate the relationships between stations.

22. What type of drawing is shown in the illustration?

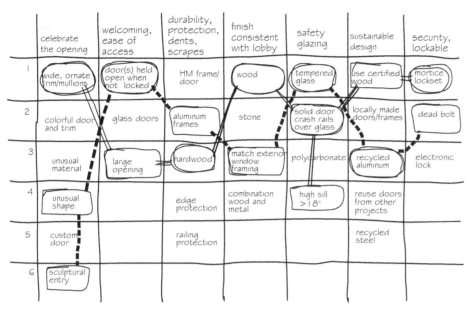

Entry to bar from lobby

(A) alternatives diagram

(B) parameter study

(C) needs matrix

(D) morphological chart

The answer is D. A morphological chart is a graphical method used to explore various possible solutions to a design problem. As shown in the illustration, the various requirements of a design are listed across the top of the chart, with the number of possible solutions along the left column. These are combined in various ways to suggest a physical response to the issue at hand—in this case, how an entrance to a bar from a hotel lobby should be designed.

23. The overall departmental relationships within a large company planning to occupy a multistory building would MOST likely be shown in a(n)

(A) block diagram

(B) adjacency matrix

(C) stacking diagram

(D) bubble diagram

The answer is C. The company is large and will occupy a multistory building and therefore multiple floors. To show overall departmental relationships (rather than individual space relationships), a stacking diagram is used. Then, individual block diagrams or bubble diagrams are developed for each floor.

24. Consider the following drawing.

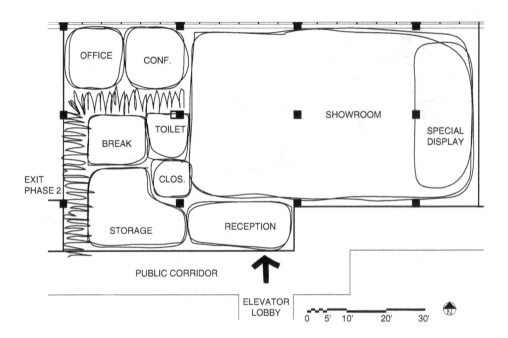

The drawing shown would typically be developed between the

(A) bubble diagram and block diagram

(B) bubble diagram and final schematic space plan

(C) concept diagram and design development plan

(D) concept diagram and final schematic space plan

The answer is D. The drawing shows a block diagram, which is used as a transition-type diagram. The block diagram is typically developed after a concept diagram and before a final schematic space plan, which shows a hardline drawing of a floor plan. At this stage of a project's schematic planning process, a block diagram identifies adjacencies, relative sizes of spaces, and the location of circulation, without showing the exact positions of partitions, doors, fixtures, or other details.

A concept diagram is developed based on a bubble diagram, and shows major influences and constraints on the design as well as the broad, overriding ideas the designer wants to incorporate into the project. A final schematic plan is developed from the block diagram and shows the exact positions of partitions, doors, plumbing fixtures, millwork, and other features that will later be developed into a design development plan.

25. A designer is hired by a large corporation for its new headquarters. The designer estimates that the corporation needs approximately 73,000 ft² of net space for its new facility. The corporation has leased three floors of 30,000 ft² each. The designer needs to program the facility, assign specific areas for each space, and assist in assigning spaces more or less equally to the various floors. The best tool for the designer to use for this task would be

(A)   a hierarchical list

(B)   an outline format

(C)   a process diagram

(D)   a spreadsheet

The answer is D.   To show a large number of individual spaces with attached floor areas and to make a summation for floor totals, a spreadsheet would be ideal. The spreadsheet's functions could accurately sum the areas, and the designer could also perform "what if" scenarios to move various spaces to each of the three floors to balance out the distribution of areas.

An outline format would be cumbersome and time consuming, and would not easily show how spaces could be assigned to the three different floors. A process diagram is not used to show a summary of spaces. A hierarchical list could be used to show the assignment of individual rooms and spaces to larger departments, but would not have the flexibility of a spreadsheet.

26.   Consider the following diagram.

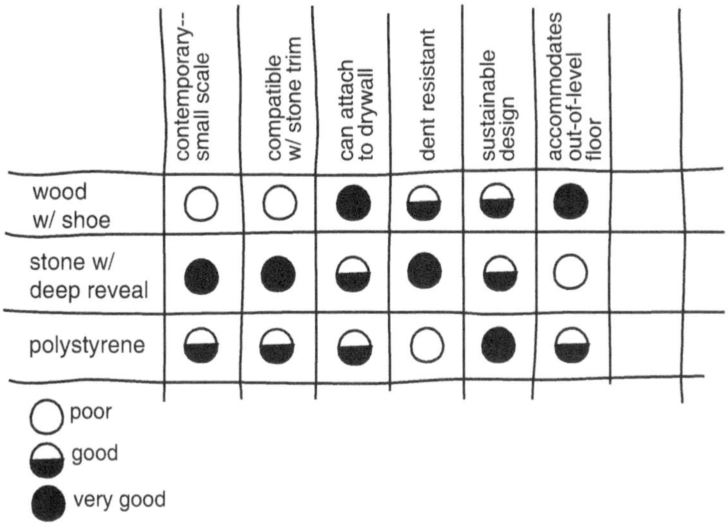

The diagram shown is an example of

(A)   a decision tree

(B)   an evaluation matrix

(C)   a materials hierarchy

(D)   a matrix chart

The answer is B. The diagram is an example of an evaluation matrix. An evaluation matrix is a good tool for analyzing alternatives of a design by looking at specific aspects of the design and giving them ratings. Ratings can be shown graphically, as in this example, or with numbers; the numbers can then be totaled to see which alternative has the best rating. The alternative with the highest ratings may be deemed to be the best choice, and a decision can be made. The evaluation matrix can be fairly simple (as this example shows) or larger and more complex for complicated design issues.

While the diagram is a matrix chart, given its grid of vertical and horizontal lines, that name doesn't describe its function for analysis and research. It also does not represent a hierarchy of materials. It is not in the form of a tree with branching alternatives, as a decision tree would be.

27. A designer is programming a large office installation that will occupy four floors in a high-rise building. In trying to determine which departments should be located on each floor, which of the following planning diagrams should the designer use?

(A) block plans
(B) bubble diagrams
(C) floor plan alternatives
(D) a stacking diagram

The answer is D. The most useful planning diagram in this situation is a stacking diagram, which is a drawing that shows the locations of major spaces or departments when a project occupies more than one floor of a multistory building. A stacking diagram based on departments or major groupings of spaces is usually worked out before each floor area is planned in detail.

Bubble diagrams show space relationships graphically as outlined by adjacency matrices, and floor plan alternatives just show possible ways programmed spaces can be laid out; neither of these relates directly to how spaces are organized floor by floor. Block plans are developed after a concept diagram and before a final schematic space plan, so the planning of which department goes on which floor should already be done by the time a block plan is developed.

28. Which of the diagrams shown might best represent a designer's concept planning for the operation and workflow of an urgent care facility?

(A)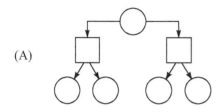

(B)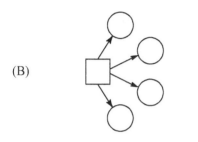

(C)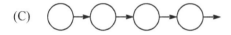

(D)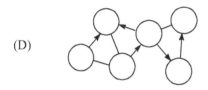

The answer is B. Option B represents a centralized organization controlling or directing other groups. This would be appropriate for an urgent care facility where the entry/reception area is the starting point for directing patients to other parts of the facility.

Option A represents a departmental organization with one person or department in the lead and other departments and groups organized below it. Option C is a linear organization where there is a starting point and subsequent activities occur in a strict sequence, which is not how an urgent care facility would operate. Option D is a network organization where activities may occur in many directions from any given starting point.

29. The adjacency diagram shown is used for space planning for an executive group.

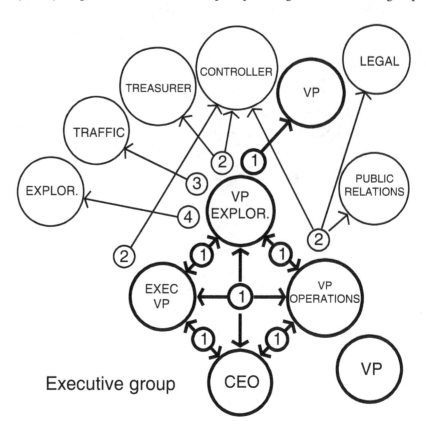

Which personnel should be located closest to the VP of exploration? (Choose the three that apply.)

(A) CEO

(B) controller

(C) traffic

(D) treasurer

(E) executive VP

(F) VP of operations

The answer is A, E, and F. In the adjacency diagram, the heavy lines and the number "1" indicate a primary relationship. The CEO, executive VP, and VP of operations are linked to the VP of exploration in this way in the diagram, so they should be located the closest.

30. Consider the drawings shown.

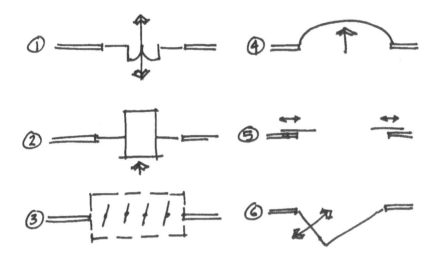

These kinds of drawings are known as

(A)   circulation components

(B)   parti diagrams

(C)   plan sketches

(D)   programmatic concepts

The answer is B.   A parti diagram is a rough drawing or diagram used early in the schematic design process to represent a design concept. The diagrams shown are concept alternatives for ways to design an entry to a bar area from a hotel lobby and are an example of a parti diagram.

There is no such type of diagram as a circulation component. These diagrams also don't represent plan sketches, nor do they show programmatic concepts, which are typically text descriptions of a programmatic idea.

❹ LIFE SAFETY AND UNIVERSAL DESIGN

31. Which of the following corridor elements must be finalized with the floor plan during design development?

(A)   floor surface material, turnaround space, and recesses for drinking fountains

(B)   corridor width, handrail projection, and exit sign locations

(C)   door swings, recesses for drinking fountains, and corridor width

(D)   location of visual alarms, turnaround space, and door swings

The answer is C.   During design development, the corridor configuration must be finalized to meet accessibility and code requirements. For this to happen, elements that can influence the width and layout of corridors must be finalized. These elements include protruding objects, door swings into the corridor, and recesses for anything that could interfere with the accessible route.

While decisions regarding elements such as floor surfacing, exit sign locations, and the location of visual alarms may be important to the final construction drawings, these elements can be finalized in the construction drawing phase and are not required during design development.

32. In a plenum, how can a fire be prevented from spreading horizontally?

(A)   Install sprinkler systems.

(B)   Use fire-rated dividers.

(C)   Use fiberglass material.

(D)   Install fire dampers.

The answer is B.   In the space between a suspended ceiling and the structural floor above, fire-rated dividers are required if partitions do not extend through the plenum. Fire dampers are used in partitions and other fire-rated separations to allow fire-rated openings for duct work.

33. What construction should be used to enclose a 1-hour-rated corridor?

(A) $^1/_2$ in (13 mm) Type X gypsum wallboard on $3^5/_8$ in (92 mm) metal studs

(B) $^5/_8$ in (16 mm) Type X gypsum wallboard on $3^5/_8$ in (92 mm) metal studs

(C)   two layers of $^1/_2$ in (13 mm) Type X gypsum wallboard on $2^1/_2$ in (64 mm) metal studs

(D) $^3/_4$ in (19 mm) gypsum wallboard on $3^5/_8$ in (92 mm) metal studs

The answer is B.   Although there are several ways to achieve a 1-hour rating, a single layer of $^5/_8$ in (16 mm) Type X wallboard is the easiest and least expensive. The size of the studs is not a critical variable. Two layers of $^1/_2$ in (13 mm) wallboard or the special $^3/_4$ in (19 mm) rated wallboard would work, but these are more than is required. $^1/_2$ in (13 mm) Type X wallboard can only achieve a 45-minute rating unless there is a veneer finish.

34. The MOST appropriate time to determine the exact requirements for grab bars in a building's toilet rooms is during which project phase?

(A)   programming

(B)   schematic design

(C)   design development

(D)   construction drawing development

The answer is C.   Only broad planning issues related to barrier-free design need to be made during the early design phases of programming and schematic design. While decisions about detailed items, like the locations of grab bars, can be made during the construction documents phase, it is better if they have been settled before the construction drawings are begun.

35. Where are flame-spread ratings in a building MOST restrictive?

    (A)   in exit enclosures

    (B)   on corridor floors

    (C)   in access ways to exits

    (D)   in enclosed spaces

The answer is A. Exit enclosures, such as stairways and exit passageways, are the most critical part of the egress system. Therefore, they must have the most restrictive flame-spread ratings.

36. When selecting interior partition finishes to meet flame-spread standards, the MOST important considerations are

    (A)   the occupancy group and the location in the building where the finishes will be used

    (B)   whether or not the building has an automatic sprinkler system and the construction type

    (C)   whether or not the partition is a fire barrier and the ratings of assemblies in the partition

    (D)   the hourly rating of the partition on which the finish will be installed and the construction type

The answer is A. Building codes limit flammability of finishes based on the occupancy of the building and whether the finishes are in an exit or not. A sprinkler system may allow a reduction in one flame-spread class rating but is not the overriding variable. Flame-spread requirements are also independent of the rating of the assembly on which the finishes are placed.

37. Working under the IBC, a designer has calculated that a total exit width of 8 ft (2 m) is required from a store. What combination of door widths would meet most exiting requirements?

    (A)   one 36 in (915 mm) door remotely located from a pair of 34 in (864 mm) doors

    (B)   a pair of 32 in (813 mm) doors remotely located from one 38 in (965 mm) door

    (C)   three 34 in (864 mm) doors remotely located

    (D)   three 36 in (915 mm) doors remotely located

The answer is D. Options A, B, and C include doors that would provide less than a clear 32 in (813 mm) wide opening.

38. In a 90,000 ft² (8360 m²), single-story office building, what would be of greatest concern in space planning?

    (A)   dead-end corridors

    (B)   corridor widths

    (C)   horizontal exits

    (D)   travel distances

The answer is D. A 90,000 ft² (8360 m²) building would be approximately 300 ft (91 m) on a side or about 250 ft (76 m) wide and 360 ft (110 m) long. The size combined with typical rectangular planning of corridors would create very long distances to exits.

39. An interior designer's client wants to remodel a one-story office building into a restaurant and nightclub. Under the IBC, the life safety of the building that will require the MOST significant change is the

(A) number and location of smoke detectors
(B) capacity of the sprinkler system
(C) size and number of exits
(D) addition of a smoke control system

The answer is C. With a change of occupancy from an office that was originally a B occupancy designed using an occupant load of 100 ft² (9.29 m²) per occupant to an assembly occupancy, A, with an occupant load of 5 ft² (0.46 m²) (standing space for a nightclub) to 15 ft² (1.39 m²) per occupant (for a restaurant with tables and chairs), the size of exits will have to be enlarged to accommodate more people. This could require major changes to the size and possibly the number and location of exits.

While additional smoke detectors and their precise locations are important, they do not represent a significant change to the building. Both offices and restaurants are considered light hazard occupancies for the purpose of designing the sprinkler system, so the overall capacity would not be affected, just the exact location of sprinkler heads once the floor plan is established. For a one-story building of assembly occupancy, a smoke control system is not needed, as it is in a large high-rise building or a building with an atrium.

40. Which of the following statements are true about fire-rated door assemblies? (Choose the four that apply.)

(A) Either hinges or rated pivots may be used.
(B) Glass area is limited based on rating.
(C) Under some circumstances, a closer is not needed.
(D) Doors must be the hollow metal type.
(E) Ball bearing steel hinges are required.
(F) Labeling is required for both the door and frame.

The answer is A, B, E, and F. Either hinges or rated pivots may be used, glass area is limited based on rating, ball bearing steel hinges are required, and labeling is required for both the door and frame.

Closers are always required at fire-rated door assemblies (protected openings). While doors with higher fire ratings (greater than 1 hour) are generally hollow metal, wood doors are available with fire ratings of less than 90 minutes.

41. When considering the initial space planning of an accessible toilet room, which of the following design elements should be of MOST concern?

(A) door swing and toilet position

(B) grab bar location and approach dimension

(C) stall depth and grab bar location

(D) door swing and approach dimension

The answer is D. The size of accessible stalls, whether standard or end-of-row type, is fixed. Factors that could affect the total space required would be use of an in-swing door (which adds to the area required) and whether the design uses a side or front approach (latch side takes the least room). Refer to the following illustration. Grab bar locations and the toilet position relative to the stall are fixed and would not be of initial concern.

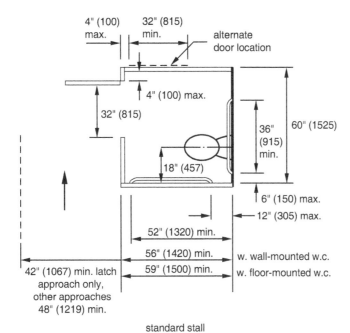

standard stall

standard stall (end of row)

42. In the detail shown, which dimension of the transition strip needs to be changed to meet accessibility requirements?

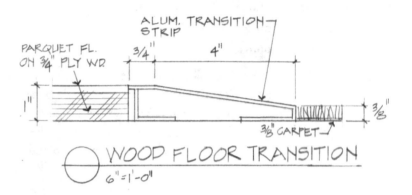

(A)   ⅜ in (9.6 mm)

(B)   ¾ in (19 mm)

(C)   1 in (25.4 mm)

(D)   4 in (101.6 mm)

The answer is D. The 4 in (101.6 mm) dimension needs to be changed. The ⅜ in (9.6 mm) carpet pile height leaves a vertical change in level of ⅝ in (15.9 mm), which must be accommodated with a ramp slope of 1:12. Either the height of the leading edge of the transition strip needs to be increased or the width of the sloped portion of the strip needs to be widened. Increasing the height of the leading edge of the transition strip to ⅝ in (15.9 mm) with a ⅜ in (9.6 mm) pile height results in an acceptable ¼ in (6.4 mm) vertical change of level from the top of the carpet to the strip, leaving a distance to the top of the wood floor of ⅜ in (9.6 mm). However, this is unrealistic because the carpet will be crushed under the weight of a wheelchair, effectively making the vertical change in level greater than ¼ in (6.4 mm). If the ⅜ in (9.6 mm) dimension remains unchanged in order to create a slope of 1:12, the width of the strip has to be widened from 4 in (101.6 mm) to 7½ in (190.5 mm) to create a 1:12 slope.

$$⅝ \text{ in } (15.9 \text{ mm}) \times 12 = 7½ \text{ in } (190.5 \text{ mm})$$

The ¾ in (19 mm) dimension is horizontal and has nothing to do with accessibility. The 1 in (25.4 mm) dimension is fixed by the thickness of the wood floor. While the Americans with Disabilities Act (ADA) allows for a change of level up to ½ in (12.7 mm), with ¼ in (6.4 mm) being vertical and ¼ in (6.4 mm) having a slope of 1:2, this approach is not possible with the given thicknesses of the carpet and the wood floor.

43. What are the MOST important design elements to incorporate into a hotel to provide safe egress for people with physical disabilities?

(A) visual alarms and audible alarms

(B) visual alarms and flashing smoke detectors

(C) audible alarms and large emergency lettering

(D) audible alarms and tactile signage

The answer is A. Emergency warning systems must provide both visual and audible alarms.

44. Based on *ANSI/ASHRAE/IESNA Standard 90.1, Energy Standard for Buildings Except Low-Rise Residential Buildings*, which method is the MOST direct and easiest to use to determine the maximum allowable lighting power density (LPD)?

(A) space-by-space method

(B) lighting system method

(C) building area method

(D) energy cost budget method

The answer is C. The building area method gives the maximum allowed power in Watts per square foot (square meter) of building area based on the building type. The power per square foot is multiplied by the gross floor area of the building to determine the LPD. This is the most direct way to determine the LPD.

The space-by-space method requires the interior designer to determine the gross area of each space type in a project and multiply that by the allowable wattage per square foot (square meter). There is no such method as the lighting system method. The energy cost budget method requires a computer simulation, which is the most complex of the given methods.

45. During space planning, the designer must locate a 36 in (915 mm) door leading from a corridor, where limited space is available, into another room. One option is to orient the corridor either perpendicular or parallel to the wall separating the corridor from the room and to swing the door in any direction. The door will have a latch only, with no closer. In order to provide for accessibility and minimize the width of the corridor, which of the following door orientations and approach directions would BEST meet the criteria?

(A) front approach, door swings into room

(B) latch side approach, door swings into corridor

(C) hinge side approach, door swings into room

(D) front approach, door swings into corridor

The answer is C. Looking at the required maneuvering clearances shown in *Illustration for Solution 45*, it is clear that the side approach with the door swinging into the room only requires a minimum of 42 in (1065 mm) (assuming the door has no closer). This would allow the use of a 44 in (1118 mm) minimum corridor. The front approach (door swings into room) and latch side approach (door swings into corridor) both require a minimum of 48 in (1220 mm). The front approach (door swings into corridor) would require a 60 in (1525 mm) corridor (a 36 in door plus 24 in of side clearance [915 mm plus 610 mm]).

Illustration for Solution 45

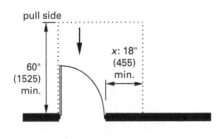
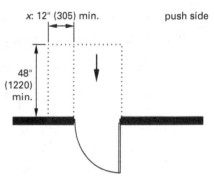

Note: *x* = 12" (305) if door has both closer and latch.

front approaches—swinging doors

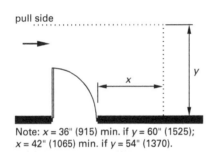

Note: *x* = 36" (915) min. if *y* = 60" (1525); *x* = 42" (1065) min. if *y* = 54" (1370).

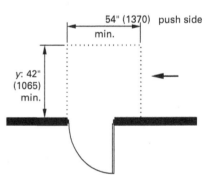

Note: *y* = 48" (1220) min. if door has both latch and closer.

hinge side approaches—swinging doors

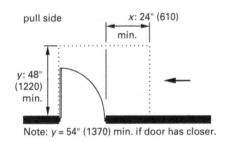

Note: *y* = 54" (1370) min. if door has closer.

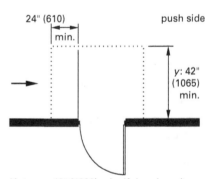

Note: *y* = 48" (1220) min. if door has closer.

latch side approaches—swinging doors

46. The interior designer is responsible for which of the following life safety considerations? (Choose the four that apply.)

(A) maintaining compartmentation according to the original architect's plans
(B) planning for an exhaust system in the remodeled spaces
(C) locating fire extinguishers as required by the local fire code
(D) specifying gaskets and closers on fire doors
(E) including fire protection of structural members according to the building type
(F) locating fire dampers in new ductwork where fire partitions have been located

The answer is A, C, D, and E. The interior designer is responsible for maintaining compartmentation, locating fire extinguishers, specifying gaskets and closers on fire doors, and including fire protection of structural members. The mechanical engineer is responsible for any exhaust system, if one is required. The mechanical engineer is also responsible for locating and specifying fire dampers, but the placement of these items is based on the location of any fire separations determined by the interior designer.

47. On a large hotel project, the interior designer is collaborating with the architect and other consultants. In reviewing preliminary drawings of the consultants to finalize the reflected ceiling plans, where should the designer look to find required fire detection and alarm locations?

(A) electrical plans
(B) electrical drawings schedules
(C) fire protection drawings
(D) mechanical plans

The answer is C. On a large project, there are separate fire protection drawings that show fire detection and alarms, as well as sprinkler plans. On a larger project, electrical plans generally do not show the fire detection and alarm locations, but they may show electrical service to them. Neither the schedules nor the mechanical plans show the fire detection and alarm locations.

48. Door fire ratings are typically given in the

(A) floor plan
(B) door elevations
(C) door schedule
(D) specifications

The answer is C. A schedule shows data in the rows and columns of a table. The door schedule includes a column in which to indicate what fire rating (in hours or minutes) is required for each door. If no rating is required, the space is left blank or filled with a dash or a zero.

49. A designer can MOST improve the safety of a restaurant's design by

(A) making the exits highly visible

(B) maintaining adequate spacing between tables

(C) avoiding a level change of one or two steps

(D) keeping the entrance to the kitchen away from seating

The answer is C. While all the options are important in developing a safe restaurant design, a level change of just one or two steps is especially dangerous for any public space that will be used by people with a wide variety of physical abilities and limitations. Steps are also dangerous for servers carrying food.

50. What is one feature of inclusive design that differentiates it from accessibility and universal design?

(A) conforms to ADA requirements

(B) considers cultural and social needs

(C) does not include a broad range of diversity

(D) responds to a broad range of users

The answer is B. Inclusive design as it relates to architecture and interior design is the design of environments and products in such a way that a diverse variety of people can use them. It also considers cultural, social, and other needs that extend beyond those of the typical user.

Inclusive design includes accessibility, but it extends design solutions not just to people with disabilities but to all users, accommodating a broad spectrum of diverse needs.

Universal design seeks to make the same design features useful to a broad range of people, including people with disabilities. For example, using a lever handle on a door serves people with disabilities but also makes it easier for all people to use. Inclusive design differs, however, in that it may involve different solutions or different groups rather than just one solution to accommodate everyone.

❺ INTERIOR BUILDING MATERIALS AND FINISHES

51. Prior to determining the preferred location of luminaires, the interior designer is reviewing the mechanical engineer's HVAC layout, as shown in the partial plan in the illustration. If there is a conflict in position between a luminaire and ductwork, which ductwork would be the easiest and least expensive to relocate?

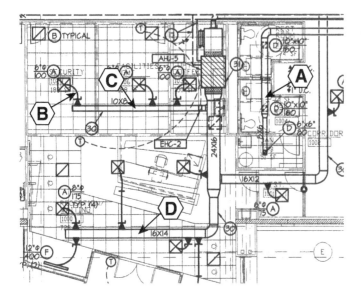

(A) duct A

(B) duct B

(C) duct C

(D) duct D

The answer is B. Duct B is a flexible duct and could be pushed out of the way or relocated easily along with the supply air diffuser to which it is attached. Duct A is a small duct for the exhaust fans in the janitor closet and the restrooms. Duct C is an 8 in × 10 in (203 mm × 254 mm) rigid duct and would be only moderately easy to relocate. Duct D is a larger rigid duct and would be difficult to move.

52. The construction assembly shown would be BEST for controlling which of the following kinds of acoustic situations?

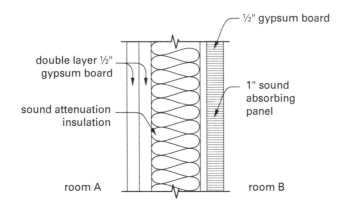

(A) impact noise

(B) transmission from room A to room B

(C) transmission from room B to room A

(D) mechanical vibration

The answer is B. The assembly shown would not be the best for controlling impact noise (because it is a partition) or mechanical vibration, so options A and D are incorrect. Although the partition construction shown would be good for preventing sound transmission in both directions, it would be *better* from room A to room B. This is because noise transmission between two rooms is dependent on the transmission loss of the wall, the area of the wall, and the absorption of the surfaces in the *receiving* room.

53. On the illustration shown, place the building elements in the correct positions on the concrete slab to provide a sand cushion terrazzo floor. Some elements may not be required.

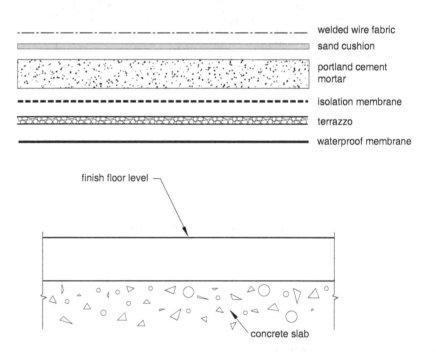

The answer is as follows. The illustration shows the correct position of the elements in this floor assembly. The sand is placed directly on the concrete slab to act as a cushion for the floor finish. The isolation membrane is placed on top of the sand and allows the concrete slab and terrazzo to move independently, minimizing cracking of the terrazzo. The portland cement mortar is poured on top of the isolation membrane and is reinforced with welded wire fabric; the thickness of the bed may be varied to allow the floor to slope to a drain. Finally, the terrazzo is placed on top. A waterproof membrane is not used in this assembly.

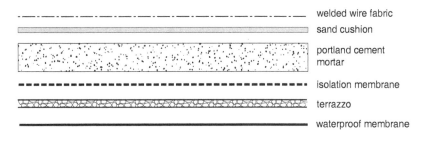

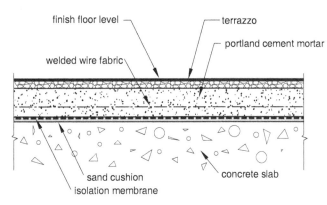

54. What ratings are the MOST important in evaluating the acoustic quality of a floor and ceiling assembly?

(A) STC and NRC

(B) IIC and STC

(C) NRC and IIC

(D) IIC and NC

The answer is B. Impact isolation class (IIC) and sound transmission coefficient (STC) are both important ratings for evaluating transmission loss through a floor and ceiling assembly.

55. Changing a ceiling from gypsum wallboard to acoustic tile would MOST affect the room's

(A) reverberation time

(B) sound transmission

(C) decibel loss

(D) impact insulation class

The answer is A. Changing from wallboard to acoustic tile affects the total absorption of a room and thereby changes the reverberation time.

56. When selecting paint for a hospital, which of the following characteristics is MOST important?

(A) abrasion resistance

(B) chemical resistance

(C) flammability

(D) VOC emissions

The answer is D. Of the characteristics provided, volatile organic compound (VOC) emissions are the most important to consider when choosing interior paint for a hospital. Paints, varnishes, carpets, adhesives, and other household products can emit VOC gases, which have a variety of short- and long-term adverse health effects, such as headaches, fatigue, dizziness, or liver and kidney damage. In all indoor environments, but especially in healthcare facilities, products with low VOC emissions should be used.

Where abrasion resistance is an important consideration, a finish other than paint should be used. Chemical resistant paint is a specially formulated finish that is unaffected by chemicals; for most hospitals, chemical staining is not an issue. Water-based paint is not flammable.

57. Which of the following are effective strategies for controlling moisture when detailing the area around a spa pool? (Choose the four that apply.)

(A) adhesives

(B) drainage

(C) slip resistance

(D) flashing

(E) tile selection

(F) sealants

The answer is B, D, E, and F. Drainage, flashing, tile selection, and sealants must be used correctly to prevent penetration of water to the substrates. Material selection must include impervious tile. Although the correct selection of adhesives and flooring materials with appropriate slip resistance ratings is important, these choices do not directly affect moisture control.

58. A designer wants to select a floor covering that is sustainable and resilient, and offers acoustical control. What flooring material BEST meets these criteria?

(A) cork

(B) linoleum

(C) vinyl tile

(D) wood parquet

The answer is A. Cork is a sustainable material, is soft underfoot, and provides the best acoustical control of the four options listed. Linoleum is a sustainable material and a resilient type of floor covering, but would not provide the best acoustical control of the four options. Vinyl tile is also resilient, but it is not a sustainable material. Wood parquet can be a sustainable material, but is hard underfoot and reflective of sound.

59. Which vinyl wall covering should be recommended for the family room in a single-family dwelling?

(A) Type I

(B) Type II

(C) Type III

(D) Type IV

The answer is A. Type I vinyl wall covering is the lightest weight of the three types and is appropriate for residential use. There is no Type IV wall covering.

60. Which carpet type allows a complex, custom-patterned carpet with varying pile heights?

(A) tufted

(B) Axminster

(C) Wilton

(D) velvet

The answer is C. Both the Axminster and Wilton processes allow for complex patterns, but only the Wilton process allows for varying pile heights.

❻ TECHNICAL SPECIFICATIONS FOR FURNITURE, FIXTURES, & EQUIPMENT AND LIGHTING

61. In designing a room in which work will take place both at video display terminals and at standard work surfaces at each individual workstation, what approach to lighting design would be MOST appropriate?

(A) Use indirect ambient lighting, and use individual task lights at each workstation.

(B) Locate downlights over work surfaces, and use indirect lighting fixtures over the terminals.

(C) Use low-brightness troffers controlled by dimmers, and use task lighting on the work surfaces.

(D) Specify a direct-indirect system that is locally controlled at each workstation.

The answer is A. Any design with provided direct lighting, as in options B, C, and D, might result in reflections off the screens. Because the question does not state that the video display terminals are in known locations, an ambient/task light system is best.

62. Which type of seaming is the MOST appropriate for upholstered furniture in a smoking lounge?

(A) channeling

(B) buttoning

(C) railroading

(D) welt cording

The answer is C. When smoldering resistance, sometimes referred to as cigarette ignition resistance, is a high priority (such as in a smoking lounge), railroad seaming should be used. Railroading is the application of fabric to furniture so that there are no intermediate seam details where cigarettes could lodge and ignite. Dropped cigarettes can easily lodge and ignite in channeling, buttoning, and welt cording seams; therefore, they should not be used.

63. Which furniture test requires that an actual piece of furniture, or an accurate full-size mockup, be tested for flammability in a large furnace?

(A) CAL TB 116

(B) CAL TB 117

(C) CAL TB 129

(D) CAL TB 133

The answer is D. California Technical Bulletin (CAL TB) 133, similar to National Fire Protection Association (NFPA) 266, requires an actual sample of furniture, or an accurate mockup of it, be tested for flammability in a large furnace. CAL TB 116 and CAL TB 117 test the cigarette ignition resistance of upholstered furniture and only require samples of furniture upholstery components. CAL TB 129 tests the flammability of mattresses.

64. What MOST affects the flammability of upholstery?

(A) type of chemical retardant used

(B) cushioning and surface fabric

(C) surface fabric and interliner

(D) surface fabric

The answer is B. Although chemical retardants and interliners are important considerations in upholstery flammability resistance, the combination of surface fabric and cushioning has the greatest effect.

65. What type of lighting system would be the most appropriate for a call center where each employee works in front of a bank of computer monitors?

(A) direct-indirect

(B) general diffuse

(C) semi-indirect

(D) indirect

The answer is D. An indirect lighting system, where all the ambient light is directed upward and reflected off the ceiling, would provide the most uniform lighting with no hot spots, and would minimize glare. Any system that directs light downward has the potential for creating glare on a reflective surface, reducing visibility and causing eye strain. Options A, B, and C would all create this condition.

66. When selecting a sofa for a residential family room, an interior designer is generally most concerned with which of the following? (Choose the four that apply.)

    (A) fabric color
    (B) fabric type
    (C) cushion density
    (D) tufting pattern
    (E) flame-retardant composition
    (F) bacterial resistance

    The answer is A, B, C, and E. An interior designer who is choosing a sofa for a residential family room would be most concerned with the sofa's color, durability, cleanability, health implications, and flammability, all of which are influenced by the type of fabric selected. Cushion density affects the durability of the sofa. While bacterial resistance may be important in commercial installations, such as a hospital or doctor's office, it would be of minor concern in a residential setting. The type of flame retardant used can have health implications. In most cases, the tufting pattern in a residential family room does not directly affect any of these, so this would be of least concern to the designer.

67. When a fabric has been fire-retardant treated, it will

    (A) resist ignition
    (B) not burn
    (C) contribute to smoke inhibition
    (D) have a lower flame spread

    The answer is B. A fire-retardant (or flame-retardant) treated fabric may ignite, but it will not support burning.

68. What types of lamps would be best to use in the display cases inside a jewelry store? (Choose the three that apply.)

    (A) 75W PAR quartz
    (B) 150W R quartz
    (C) 14W T5 fluorescent
    (D) 90W MR-16
    (E) 40W T10
    (F) 20W LED

The answer is C, D, and F. There are two aspects to consider for this application: size and color rendition. T5 fluorescent lamps can be specified with a high color temperature and are small enough to fit within most types of display cases. MR-16 lamps are relatively small and are tungsten-halogen lamps that would provide good color rendition and sparkle to jewelry. Light-emitting diode (LED) lamps would be the best choice because of their small size, cool operating temperature, and availability in a variety of color outputs.

Both the 75W parabolic aluminized reflector (PAR) and 150W reflector (R) lamps would be too large to use in a display case and would generate a great deal of heat. A 40W T10 would be small enough to use in the display case, but its incandescent color rendition would be too warm for jewelry display.

69. An interior designer has just finished reviewing the plans for a large office suite when the building department states that the lighting budget has been exceeded. If the design is composed of 80% fluorescent lighting and 20% incandescent lighting, what is the BEST course of action to begin redesign?

(A)   Reduce the number of luminaires by spacing them farther apart.

(B)   Substitute all incandescent lights with fluorescent lights.

(C)   Change to a task-ambient lighting system.

(D)   Investigate whether lamps with higher efficacies will bring the design within the budget.

The answer is D. Option D allows everything but the lamps to be left unchanged. If this investigation did not bring the design within the budget, then the other options consistent with the design could be explored. Option A is not the best action because the illumination can easily be lowered below an acceptable level. Option B is a possibility and may ultimately be necessary, but other options should be explored first because the question asks what should be done to begin redesign. Option C is also a possibility, but the original design was developed for a reason and the first action should be to try to make that work.

70. What type of cushioning would be BEST for a hospital waiting room?

(A)   high-density foam

(B)   cotton batting

(C)   combustion-modified foam with a low ILD

(D)   low-density polyurethane

The answer is A. High-density foam is used to create firm cushions. Firmer cushions prevent fabric coverings from stretching, thereby extending their useful life and appearance from the constant and heavy use of a hospital's waiting room.

Cotton batting and low-density polyurethane are not as durable as high-density foam, and any material with a low indentation load deflection (ILD) implies a soft cushion (which is also much less durable than a firm cushion).

71. To confirm that a particular project meets material flammability requirements, an interior designer should

(A) contact each manufacturer whose materials are used

(B) refer to state flammability regulations

(C) contact the authority having jurisdiction (AHJ)

(D) review the *International Building Code* (IBC)

The answer is C. Although there are flammability requirements in the IBC and in state regulations, the jurisdiction in which the project is located may have additional requirements. For this reason, it is necessary to contact the authority having jurisdiction.

72. Smoke detector locations are shown on the

(A) floor plan only

(B) reflected ceiling plan only

(C) electrical plan only

(D) reflected ceiling plan and electrical plan

The answer is D. The electrical engineer is responsible for locating and circuiting smoke detectors, which are shown on the electrical plan. Smoke detectors are also shown on the interior designer's reflected ceiling plan so that the designer can coordinate them with other ceiling-mounted objects.

73. Which standard of the Business and Institutional Furniture Manufacturers Association (BIFMA) establishes criteria for the sustainability of furniture?

(A) ANSI/BIFMA e3

(B) ANSI/BIFMA G1

(C) ANSI/BIFMA M7.1

(D) ANSI/BIFMA/SOHO S6.5

The answer is A. ANSI/BIFMA e3, *Furniture Sustainability Standard*, provides performance criteria addressing environmental and social impacts throughout the supply chain of furniture, as well as product-based characteristics that impact the environment, health and wellness, and society.

ANSI/BIFMA G1, *Ergonomics Guideline for Furniture Used in Office Work Spaces Designed for Computer Use*, provides guidelines for furniture intended for computer use by applying measurable principles and design requirements.

ANSI/BIFMA M7.1, *Testing for VOC Emissions from Office Furniture and Seating*, provides manufacturers, specifiers, and users with a basis for characterizing the initial release of various airborne chemicals emitted from a furniture workstation and seating.

ANSI/BIFMA/SOHO S6.5, *Small Office/Home Office Furniture—Tests*, provides performance and safety requirements for storage and desk furniture intended for use in the small office and home office.

74. An interior designer is selecting lamps for a residential living room. What color temperature should the designer select to create a warm, comfortable atmosphere?

(A) 2700K

(B) 4300K

(C) 6500K

(D) 7500K

The answer is A. Color temperature, which is measured in kelvins (K), is the temperature to which a black body radiator would have to be heated to produce that color. The lower the temperature, the "warmer" or redder the apparent color is. A color temperature of 2700K would be good to create a warm atmosphere.

4300K is the color of a cool white fluorescent lamp, while a color temperature of 6500K is the color of a daylight fluorescent. An overcast sky has a color temperature of about 7500K. All of these would have more of a blue or "cool" component.

75. Which of the following would be the best source for looking at items just introduced to the furniture industry?

(A) industry magazine advertisements

(B) local dealer showrooms

(C) merchandise marts

(D) trade shows

The answer is D. Trades shows are typically events where new furniture items are introduced to the industry. They are excellent places to see actual examples of the furniture and to talk to the manufacturers about costs and technical specifications. Local dealer showrooms and merchandise marts usually lag a little behind trade shows in making new items accessible. Magazine advertisements may show previews of what will be shown at the trade shows, but they cannot take the place of seeing the real thing and being able to sit on it or touch it.

❼ CONSTRUCTION DRAWINGS, SCHEDULES, AND SPECIFICATIONS

76. In working with an electrical engineer on a project, what information would the designer MOST likely put on the interior design power plan?

(A) switch locations

(B) dedicated outlets

(C) conduit sizing

(D) speaker locations

The answer is B. The interior designer would not determine conduit size or put speaker locations on the power plan. This eliminates options C and D. Switch locations would be placed on the reflected ceiling plan.

77. Which type of drawing would typically include the symbol shown in the illustration?

(A) floor plan

(B) reflected ceiling plan

(C) elevation

(D) section detail

The answer is A. The symbol shown is an elevation reference mark and is used on floor plans to indicate (point to) a wall surface that is shown in elevation view elsewhere on the set of drawings. The bottom number is the sheet on which the elevation is drawn, and the top number is the sequential number on that sheet.

78. Which of the following organizations would be the BEST resource for an interior designer looking for independent, third-party information on the sustainability of architectural woodwork materials?

(A) Architectural Woodwork Institute

(B) BuildingGreen

(C) Forest Stewardship Council

(D) U.S. Green Building Council

The answer is B. BuildingGreen is an independent publisher offering unbiased information on sustainable building design and product information. It publishes *Environmental Building News*, a monthly newsletter, and the *GreenSpec Directory*, which lists product information for sustainable materials. BuildingGreen also offers various online tools on its website.

The Architectural Woodwork Institute is the primary source for standards and information about woodwork in general, but has limited data on sustainability, and generally refers people to other sources for information on that subject. The Forest Stewardship Council oversees the development of standards for forest management principles; these standards cover all types of wood products, not specifically sustainable woodwork materials. The U.S. Green Building Council establishes criteria for the certification of sustainable buildings in its LEED rating systems. Although the rating systems contain criteria for the use of wood, they are not specifically concerned with woodwork.

79. A demolition plan is required when the

(A) local authority having jurisdiction (AHJ) requires one
(B) use of an additional line type for removed items would be too confusing
(C) demolition involves partitions, doors, and cabinetry
(D) mix of new construction and demolition is too complex for one drawing

The answer is D. Demolition plans are required when the overlay of significant amounts of demolition interferes with the linework required for new construction. Local AHJs do not typically require a separate demolition plan. Using an additional line type, such as a dashed line, can be confusing if the plan is dense with linework, symbols, and notations. Whether demolition specifically involves partitions, doors, and cabinetry is not the important factor in determining if a separate plan is required.

80. When a project includes both fixed partition walls and a full-height moveable partition system, on what plan should the moveable partition system be shown?

(A) a separate moveable partition plan
(B) the construction floor plan
(C) the furniture plan
(D) both the floor and furniture plans

The answer is B. A full-height moveable partition system should be shown on the construction floor plan, along with the fixed partition walls. This is because any type of full-height partitions will affect egress, as well as the HVAC system design, lighting, and sprinkler layout. A moveable partition plan is not necessary and is not a typical type of interior design drawing. A furniture plan would show cubicles and other moveable equipment but not moveable partitions.

81. The method of constructing a fire-rated partition is typically indicated in the

(A) partition details
(B) floor plan keynotes
(C) partition schedule
(D) contract specifications

The answer is A. The partition details would indicate the method of constructing a fire-rated partition. The details include the framing, type, and thickness of gypsum wallboard or other construction, as well as how the partition's edges and other penetrations are sealed.

Floor plan keynotes indicate only a partition's fire rating, not the actual method of constructing it. Partition schedules are seldom used, and in any case, they indicate only a partition's fire rating. Although contract specifications include important information about standards, quality of construction, and other aspects of fire-rated construction, they would not show a partition's actual construction method.

82. The partial floor plan given shows the subdivision of one side of an existing building into five offices with the architectural dimensions given on the outside of the building. Why is office #305 not dimensioned?

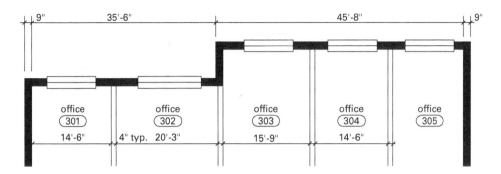

(A)   It is the same width as office #304.

(B)   Dimension strings are left incomplete.

(C)   There may be a potential conflict with the existing overall dimension.

(D)   The dimensions can be calculated by subtraction from the existing architectural dimensions.

The answer is C.   When an existing space is subdivided, the designer is relying on information gathered through onsite measurement or record drawings. The existing overall dimension may or may not be exactly what is shown on the architectural drawings. By leaving what is known as an *open dimension* in the dimension string, the undimensioned space can accommodate any slight variation between the actual dimension and that shown on the architectural plans without the contractor raising questions. The open dimension should be the space that is the least important to have exactly as dimensioned.

There is no information given on the plan that would allow the contractor to determine that an adjacent office should be the same size as another just by visual inspection (option A). Dimension strings are not necessarily left incomplete in all circumstances (option B). The contractor should not have to calculate dimensions, and in this case, the dimension of office #305 would not be accurate because the thickness of the existing exterior wall is not known.

83. When completing a set of construction drawings for a restaurant kitchen, an interior designer should include an enlarged floor plan in order to

(A)   show all kitchen equipment and reference notes

(B)   indicate detailed dimensions of the countertop layout

(C)   show all plumbing drains and hot and cold supply points

(D)   satisfy health department requirements for submitted drawings

The answer is A.   A commercial kitchen contains a complex collection of equipment, work surfaces, and plumbing. A standard ¼ in scale plan drawing probably would not be large enough to show all the equipment, dimensions, and annotation required, so a large-scale plan is typically necessary to communicate this information.

Detailed dimensions of the countertop are not the only pieces of information required for a commercial kitchen. As with countertop layout, plumbing information (option C) is not the only information required and would be included on the mechanical engineer's drawings. Health department requirements do not require an enlarged floor plan as long as all the required information is shown. In some cases—for example, for a simple kitchen layout—this may be possible with the same scale drawing as the rest of the project.

84. An interior designer is providing complete space planning and furniture, fixtures, and equipment (FF&E) specification services for a large law firm. The location of electrical, telephone, and communication outlets for the space is BEST shown on the

- (A) electrical plan
- (B) floor plan
- (C) furniture plan
- (D) power/communications plan

The answer is D. In this case, it is best to use separate power/telephone plans and furniture plans. There would then be sufficient space to dimension and annotate the outlets on one plan and sufficient space for furniture locations and annotations on the furniture plan.

The electrical plan (option A) is produced by the electrical engineer. It indicates the general locations of the outlets and shows the circuiting, conduit, and other technical information. An electrical plan does not typically include dimensions indicating where the receptacles are to be installed. For a large commercial project, the floor plan (option B) is not an appropriate place to show outlet locations because the floor plan will most likely be crowded with other information. While outlets are sometimes shown on a furniture plan (option C), for a client such as a large law firm, there would be numerous electrical, telephone, and communication outlets, as well as many furniture items. Trying to combine them and include all necessary information would result in a cluttered and difficult-to-read drawing.

85. For a project with an irregular plan and multiple wall finishes, what is the BEST method to describe finishes on the construction drawings?

- (A) Identify all finishes on a schedule.
- (B) Develop a code number for each wall that references a finish schedule.
- (C) Provide elevations as necessary and use a standard finish schedule.
- (D) Use a finish plan with codes referenced to a legend and draw elevations when required.

The answer is D. For a project with both an irregular plan (with angles, curves, and rooms with more than four walls) and multiple wall finishes on the same surface, a finish plan using lines extending the length of each finish along with a code is the best way to show where wall finishes start and stop. For walls with multiple wall finishes that may start and stop at various points above the floor, an elevation is the most accurate way to indicate finish layout.

Using a schedule where finishes are referenced by room numbers is appropriate only for projects with simple finishes and on floor plans where each room has only four walls, and all are scheduled to receive the same type and color of finish. Using code numbers for each wall would result in an excessively large amount of numbers on the plan, many of which would be unnecessarily repetitious and still could not describe single walls with multiple finishes. While interior elevations would be useful, a standard finish schedule referenced to room numbers could not easily describe an irregular plan or communicate instructions for spaces where walls are to receive different finishes.

86. On what type of drawing would the symbol shown in the illustration be used?

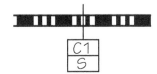

(A)   reflected ceiling plan

(B)   egress plan

(C)   construction floor plan

(D)   mechanical floor plan

The answer is C.   The drawing shows a partition type indication with an accompanying flag note. It would be used on a construction floor plan to graphically show the construction of the partition and to differentiate it from adjacent partitions of another construction type. The flag note numbers are references to a legend that would give additional information about the construction, such as its fire rating, stud size, and finish.

87. When reviewing the mechanical engineer's plan to identify the location of HVAC controls in the finished space, what symbol should the interior designer look for?

(A)

(B)

(C)

(D)

The answer is C.   The thermostat is the primary HVAC system control in the finished space, and is represented by a circle with the letter T in it. The interior designer would be concerned with this to coordinate its position with an elevation of the interior space. Option A is not a standard mechanical symbol. Option B indicates a fire damper in a duct when used on a mechanical plan, and is also the symbol for a floor telephone outlet when used on an electrical or telephone plan. Option D is the symbol for a smoke detector in the ceiling.

88. Where on the construction drawings is it MOST appropriate to indicate that corridors conform to surface requirements for accessible routes?

(A)　on the detail sections

(B)　on the elevations

(C)　on the floor plans

(D)　in the schedules

The answer is A.　The types of surfaces used in corridors, as well as minor changes in elevation such as those that may occur at thresholds and changes of material, usually must meet surface requirements for accessibility. Conformance to these requirements is best shown on the construction drawings' detail sections.

89. On the illustration shown, place the hot spot marker in the location that would make it difficult to install the glazing assembly in a level position.

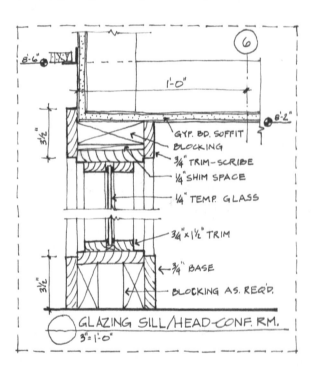

A shim space should be provided above the blocking. Shim spaces allow accurately built construction elements to fit within an opening that may not be perfectly square so it can be leveled. Shim spaces are also used to provide enough clearance to slide the element into the opening. The shaded area in the illustration indicates the margin of error for placing the hot spot marker.

The interior window assembly, including the glazing and frame, would be assembled in the woodworking shop and brought to the job site as a unit. The blocking indicated below the window assembly would follow the line of the structural floor. If there are variations in the floor slab, or variations in the thickness of the blocking members, the top of this blocking will likely not be level. Placing the finished glazed portion directly on the blocking will skew the window assembly and put it out of level.

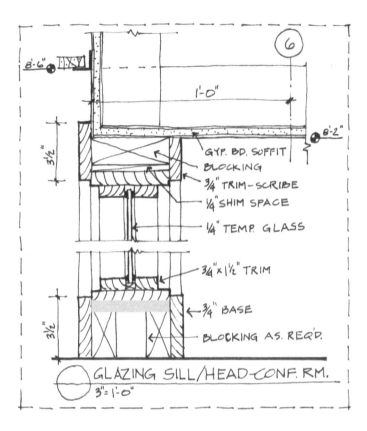

8'-6"

1'-0"

6

8'-2"

3½"

GYP. BD. SOFFIT
BLOCKING
¾" TRIM-SCRIBE
¼" SHIM SPACE
¼" TEMP. GLASS
¾" x 1½" TRIM
¾" BASE
BLOCKING AS. REQ'D.

3½"

GLAZING SILL/HEAD-CONF. RM.
3" = 1'-0"

90. The drawing shown is a sketch detail of a partial-height partition, which, in plan view, is part of a U-shaped enclosure that will be used to support and enclose a built-in stand-up work surface. What problem in construction does this detail indicate?

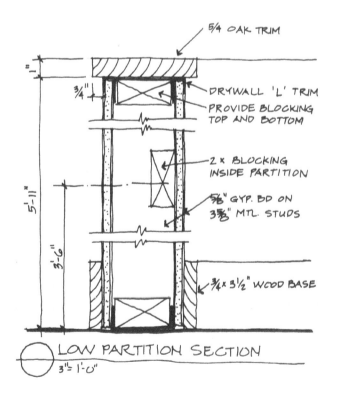

5/4 OAK TRIM

1"

¾"

DRYWALL 'L' TRIM
PROVIDE BLOCKING
TOP AND BOTTOM

2 x BLOCKING
INSIDE PARTITION

⅝" GYP. BD ON
3⅝" MTL. STUDS

5'-11"

3'-6"

¾ x 3½" WOOD BASE

LOW PARTITION SECTION
3" = 1'-0"

(A) The partition will be unstable due to its height.

(B) The 2× blocking will not provide sufficient support for the work surface.

(C) The 5/4 oak trim will be difficult to install level.

(D) There is not enough blocking to attach the wood base.

The answer is C. There is no shim space indicated below the 5/4 oak trim, so the metal stud top runner would have to be installed perfectly level, which is difficult with rough framing, so it would be difficult to install the oak trim level. Because of the U-shaped configuration and the additional bracing that the work surface will provide to the vertical elements, the partition will have sufficient stability. The 2× blocking will provide sufficient backing for the attachment of any work surface support, such as a wood cleat, on the outside of the partition. The blocking shown inside the metal stud runner would provide sufficient support for the wood base. It could even be omitted if metal stud finishing screws are used to attach the base to the partition.

91. What kind of scale is best used to measure the size of a drawn feature in feet and decimal fractions of a foot?

(A) architect's scale

(B) engineer's scale

(C) metric scale

(D) graphic scale

The answer is B. When a feature is measured with an engineer's scale, which uses scales such as $1'' = 40'$ or $1'' = 100'$, the measurement is read in feet, tenths of a foot, and hundredths of a foot. Civil engineers use scales of this type, or their CAD equivalent, to mark dimensions when drafting.

When an architect's scale is used, the measurement and subsequent dimension is read in feet and inches, not feet and decimal fractions of a foot. A metric scale is similar to an engineer's scale in that it has 10 graduations per division, but the resulting dimensions are in millimeters, centimeters, or meters, not feet and decimal fractions of a foot. A metric scale is used when a project is planned and presented with SI units. A graphic (e.g., graphical, bar, linear, map) scale is a feature printed in the legend of a map or other drawing. Its resolution is usually coarse. Where smaller than whole divisions are indicated on a graphic scale, they are generally limited to $^{1}/_{4}$, $^{1}/_{2}$, and $^{3}/_{4}$ graduations, so it would be difficult to measure the size of features in feet and decimal fractions of a foot.

92. When taking field measurements using a tape measure, what is the FASTEST way to verify accuracy?

(A) Measure each dimension twice from different directions.

(B) Have two people take the same measurements and compare.

(C) Use a laser-based device to compare with measurements taken manually.

(D) Compare a string of dimensions with the overall dimension measurement.

The answer is D. The *fastest* way is to take an overall dimension and compare it with the sum of a string of dimensions of the same elements. If the two values are close, the individual measurements are probably close enough to be used for planning and construction documents. If the values are divergent, the measurements should be taken a second time. While measuring twice and having two people take the same measurements may be good ways to check work, they are not the fastest methods for verifying the accuracy of the data. If a laser-based device is used to check measurements made by a tape measure, the laser should have been used in the first place.

93. Sharing common information in the same CAD file to create different types of drawings is known as

(A) building modeling
(B) using the drawing modules standard
(C) layering of drawings
(D) using the U.S. National CAD Standard (NCS)

The answer is C. Layering of drawings refers to the practice of placing different information on separate layers (or levels) in a CAD or BIM system. This allows individual layers to be shown or hidden as required to develop different types of drawings (floor plan, reflected ceiling plan, or furniture plan) using shared information from the same computer file.

Building modeling simply refers to a three-dimensional representation of a structure. Drawing modules refers to how individual drawings are organized on a sheet within a grid system. The U.S. NCS is a collection of drawing standards, with layering being only one of those standards.

94. What does the symbol shown in the illustration indicate?

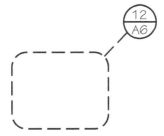

(A) The area within the bubble is drawn at a larger scale elsewhere in the drawing set.
(B) A section cut of the area in the bubble is shown on sheet A6 of the drawing set.
(C) An elevation within the bubble is shown elsewhere at a different scale.
(D) The portion within the bubble is described in more detail in the specifications.

The answer is A. The symbol shown is a detail reference mark, which can be thought of as a magnifying glass. This symbol indicates that the portion of construction within the dashed bubble is drawn at a larger scale somewhere else. In this example, a larger-scale representation of the area is shown as detail number 12 on sheet

A6 of the drawing set. This symbol indicates that the larger-scale drawing will have the same point of view; that is, if it encloses part of an elevation, the drawing referenced will still be in elevation view, just larger. It can be used on all types of drawings, including plans, elevations, and details. This is not a section-cut symbol. The symbol is not limited to just elevations and is typically used mostly for plans. This symbol does not refer to specifications.

95. Which standard is used for construction drawing sheet sizes for nongovernmental projects in the United States?

    (A)   ANSI

    (B)   architectural

    (C)   ASTM International

    (D)   ISO

The answer is B. Architectural and interior design drawings commonly use the architectural standard sizes, which begin with the size A, or 9 in × 12 in. Each sheet size larger is a multiple of that module; a B-size drawing, for example, is 12 in × 18 in, and a C-size drawing is 18 in × 24 in.

The ANSI standard is based on a module of 8.5 in × 11 in and is not commonly used. ASTM International does not have a standard for architectural sheet sizes. The ISO standard is based on a module of 210 mm × 297 mm (8.3 in × 11.7 in), and is not used in the United States.

❽ PROFESSIONAL DEVELOPMENT AND ETHICS

96. For a member of the International Interior Design Association (IIDA), which action is a clear violation of the IIDA Code of Ethics?

    (A)   advertising in trade journals showing projects that the member firm has completed

    (B)   including website photos of a project that was created by an employee while previously working for another firm

    (C)   offering support to students of interior design, including information about the firm's projects

    (D)   refusing to accept their client's instructions concerning copying a specific desired design feature the client saw in another project

The answer is B. In the section "Responsibility to Other Interior Designers and Colleagues," a professional or an associate member may only take credit for work that was actually created by the member or the member's firm. Showing previous work by an employee that was performed while working at another firm is a clear violation of the IIDA Code of Ethics.

Advertising is allowed as long as it is done without any form of false or misleading advertising or promotion. Members and associate members are encouraged to offer support, and information to students of interior design. Members may not accept instructions from their clients which knowingly involve plagiarism.

97. What is considered the primary canon of the Code of Ethics of both the American Society of Interior Designers and the International Interior Design Association?

(A) not to knowingly violate any law, regulation, or code
(B) not to withhold any financial interest the designer may have in a project
(C) to consider the health, safety, and welfare of the public
(D) to perform services in the best interest of their client

The answer is C. While all canons of the American Society of Interior Designers (ASID) and International Interior Design Association (IIDA) codes of ethics are important, the most important is to consider and protect the health, safety, and welfare of the public. An interior design member of ASID and IIDA should also always perform services in the best interest of the client; not violate any law, regulation, or code; and always disclose any financial or other interest the designer has in a project.

98. While working on a large restaurant project, an interior designer and ASID member is given a set of drawings by the client for a public seating area that another designer developed for the client's previous restaurant. The interior designer is told to incorporate them into the current project and reduce their fee. What should the designer tell the client?

(A) The drawings will be included, and the fee that was originally built into their fee proposal for developing their own seating area plans will be reduced.
(B) The drawings can be included, but the client will have to pay the original design fee for that portion of the project.
(C) The drawings cannot be used because of ethical concerns, and the designer must develop new plans and drawings for the original set fee, but will include as much of the previous design as possible.
(D) The drawings cannot directly be included in the designer's own set of documents because the designer did not prepare or supervise their development, but the designer could use them if the client paid for the extra time required to professionally review them.

The answer is D. In the section "Responsibility to the Public," the American Society of Interior Designers (ASID) Code of Ethics prohibits the designer from sealing or signing drawings or other design documents, except where the designer or designer's firm has prepared, supervised, or professionally reviewed the documents. In this case the designer did not prepare them, but the Code of Ethics allows them to use the drawings if they review them.

Options A and B are incorrect because the designer is not allowed to use the drawings directly regardless of whether the fee was reduced or remained the same. Option C is incorrect because they could use the drawings if they professionally reviewed them.

99. Which of the following activities can an interior designer engage in to fulfill their social responsibility as well as expand their professional development? (Choose the four that apply.)

(A) avoid conduct that would involve misrepresentation in professional activity

(B) develop public service announcements promoting interior designers

(C) join committees that develop or review industry standards

(D) serve on design review boards in the location where the designer practices

(E) participate in student critiques at the local interior design school

(F) volunteer time to provide public education about the profession

The answer is C, D, E, and F. Volunteering time for public education, serving on design review boards, helping to develop industry standards, and participating in student critiques are all excellent ways to give back to the community as well as to expand professional development.

Option A is part of a code of ethics and would not serve as a way to satisfy social responsibility. Option B is not really a social responsibility.

100. Which section of the International Interior Design Association's Code of Ethics requires continuing education?

(A) "Responsibility to the Association and Interior Design Profession"

(B) "Responsibility to the Client"

(C) "Responsibility to Other Interior Designers and Colleagues"

(D) "Responsibility to the Public"

The answer is A. In the section "Responsibility to the Association and Interior Design Profession," the second canon states that professional and associate members shall seek to continually upgrade their professional knowledge and competency with respect to the interior design profession. There is a similar provision in the American Society of Interior Designers Code of Ethics. Options B, C, and D are parts of the International Interior Design Association's Code of Ethics, but they do not relate to continuing education.

MOCK EXAM

Do not use reference books while taking this mock exam. Besides this book, you should have only pencils, scratch paper, and a calculator. (For the actual exam, these will be provided and should not be brought into the site.)

Exam time limit: 3.0 hours

❶ PROGRAMMING AND SITE ANALYSIS

1. According to the affinity matrix shown, to which rooms must the kitchen be adjacent? (Choose the three that apply.)

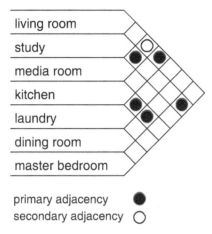

(A) living room

(B) study

(C) media room

(D) laundry

(E) dining room

(F) master bedroom

2. Which of the following is a true statement about the difference between a programmatic concept and a design concept?

(A) A design concept specifies a particular way to achieve the programmatic concept.

(B) There are many more programmatic concepts for a problem than there are design concepts.

(C) A design concept is a performance requirement.

(D) Design concepts are developed before programmatic concepts.

3. Which of the following are critical planning concerns for a commercial office space? (Choose the four that apply.)

(A) adjacencies

(B) daylighting

(C) means of egress

(D) plan type

(E) efficiency factor

(F) column locations

4. Which of the diagrams shown is best suited for making a record of required space relationships just before initial space planning?

(A)

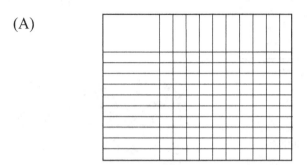

(B)

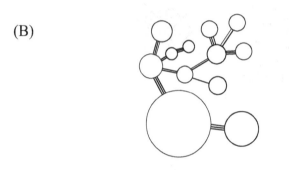

(C)

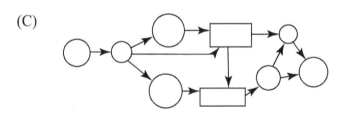

(D)

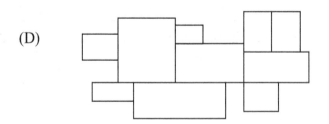

5. A restaurant in an old building is undergoing remodeling. Which of the following existing building elements would have the MOST influence over the space plan for the proposed dining area?

(A) loadbearing columns and interior walls
(B) building dimensions
(C) plumbing fixtures
(D) decorative millwork and ornate lighting fixtures

6. A designer has determined that a client needs about 8000 ft² (740 m²) of usable office space. The leasing agent for the building says that the rentable-usable ratio will be 1.25. Approximately how much area should the interior designer recommend that the client lease?

(A)   7500 ft² (700 m²)

(B)   10,000 ft² (930 m²)

(C)   10,700 ft² (1000 m²)

(D)   13,300 ft² (1200 m²)

7. When developing adjacency requirements, the interior designer must consider

(A)   contacts between people, transfer of objects, and electronic information

(B)   outside contacts with service people and visitors, as well as internal contacts

(C)   shared equipment and transfer of objects between people

(D)   frequency of required contacts between people and transfer of objects

8. The BEST way to gather programming information from workers in a large office is through

(A)   observation

(B)   questionnaires

(C)   interviews

(D)   benchmarks

9. A library is being designed to occupy only one portion of a building, and a complete set of drawings is available for the building. What information would be the MOST important to obtain from the field survey?

(A)   locations of structural elements

(B)   existing natural light sources

(C)   sources of noise within the building

(D)   locations and capacities of electrical power

10. A residential design involves a bedroom, bath, and garage addition. At a minimum, the due diligence site investigation should include

(A)   neighborhood character and zoning setbacks

(B)   zoning setbacks and septic capacities

(C)   heating system capacity and neighborhood traffic

(D)   zoning height limitations and street characteristics

11. Understanding a client's sustainability goals when looking for office space will help the interior designer

(A) determine if the project can be LEED certified

(B) review the energy conservation of the mechanical system

(C) determine if the building can be located in a brownfield site

(D) focus site analyses on features that support sustainable design

12. What existing condition in a building would MOST affect the cost of a new interior design?

(A) location of exits

(B) limited views and daylight

(C) lack of a sprinkler system

(D) remote location of an electrical closet

13. In the five-step programming process outlined by the book *Problem Seeking*, the fifth step is to state the problem. What is the order of the first four steps?

(A) determine needs, collect and analyze facts, uncover and test concepts, establish goals

(B) collect and analyze facts, determine needs, establish goals, uncover and test concepts

(C) uncover and test concepts, establish goals, determine needs, collect and analyze facts

(D) establish goals, collect and analyze facts, uncover and test concepts, determine needs

❷ RELATIONSHIP BETWEEN HUMAN BEHAVIOR AND THE DESIGNED ENVIRONMENT

14. A college dormitory room shared by two people contains two identical sets of furnishings, symmetrically positioned. Which of the following psychological needs is this arrangement attempting to satisfy?

(A) personal space

(B) territoriality

(C) group interaction

(D) personalization

15. An interior designer talking with a client could justify the use of bright colors in an elderly care facility by referring to

(A) design theory

(B) evidence from research

(C) Gestalt psychology

(D) historic precedent

16. Which of the following should an interior designer FIRST take into account when designing a church's interior?

(A) cultural attitudes

(B) proxemics

(C) regionalism

(D) symbolism

17. Proxemics would be MOST helpful to a designer who is deciding on the

(A) size of a doctor's examination room

(B) location of the office of the president within an office suite

(C) size and shape of a conference table

(D) type and spacing of seating in an audiovisual presentation room

18. An interior designer is creating the design concept for a home. In addition to satisfying the program and meeting the specific needs of the client, the designer would typically be MOST responsive to the influence of

(A) economic conditions

(B) cultural attitudes

(C) regionalism

(D) symbolism

19. A client has asked a designer to create an intimate seating area for a hospital waiting room. Which of the following will be MOST important in achieving the client's goal?

(A) pattern

(B) scale

(C) texture

(D) color

20. A designer wants to give visual weight to a sofa. Which of the following color combinations would be the BEST choice for the sofa and the surrounding walls?

(A) a hue with a dark value for the sofa and a slightly lighter value for the walls

(B) any light-colored hue for the sofa and a color with a dark value for the walls

(C) a color with a warm hue and a dark value for the sofa and a much lighter color for the walls

(D) a light, cool color for the sofa and a color of similar value and hue for the walls

21. An interior designer is creating a color-coding system for use in a housing facility for the elderly. Which of the following color combinations would be the MOST vivid and easily perceived?

(A) a bright color against a background of a noncomplementary color

(B) complementary colors of high saturation

(C) highly saturated warm or cool colors next to a neutral gray

(D) the primary colors and white

22. Which design element could be used to make a ceiling appear lower?

(A) a dark, highly textured ceiling

(B) strong horizontal lines on the walls

(C) fine-grained patterns on the ceiling and dark walls

(D) a light ceiling and textured walls

23. One basic theory about how inherent human motivation acts as a psychological influence on socialization and design is

(A) behavior setting theory

(B) proxemics

(C) McClelland's human motivation theory

(D) Maslow's hierarchy of needs

24. An interior designer is consulting with an architect for a new bariatric care facility. What does the interior designer need to be most concerned with? (Choose the four that apply.)

(A) space for health care workers around the bed

(B) chairs and other seating

(C) integration of bariatric seating with standard seating

(D) door sizes

(E) equipment storage

(F) bedside amenities such as refrigerators

25. A designer wants to emphasize one particular item in a client's retail store. Which of the following design features would BEST achieve this goal?

(A) locating the item on a main circulation axis and highlighting it

(B) arranging a grouping of several of the items among single pieces of the other items

(C) having an oversized model of the item made for display near the entrance

(D) putting the item on a brightly colored pedestal in its usual place in the store

❸ DESIGN COMMUNICATION TECHNIQUES

26. During the preliminary planning phase, the diagram shown would be used to

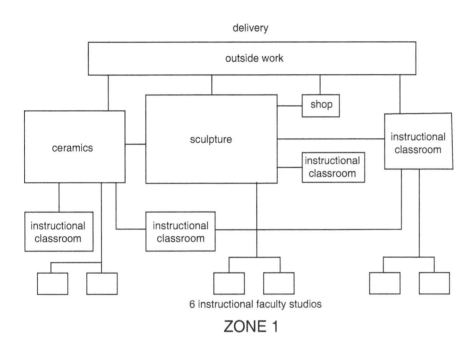

ZONE 1

(A)   help the designer present data for adjacencies and area

(B)   show the client which programmed spaces belong in this zone

(C)   determine maximum floor areas on a building floor

(D)   begin the process for developing a stacking diagram

27. A perspective drawing is the BEST type of drawing to use when presenting to a client because it

(A)   is the quickest method of rendering space

(B)   most accurately shows vertical dimensions relative to the viewer

(C)   is most like the way space and objects are actually perceived

(D)   offers the widest choice of viewpoints

28. The illustration shown represents a(n)

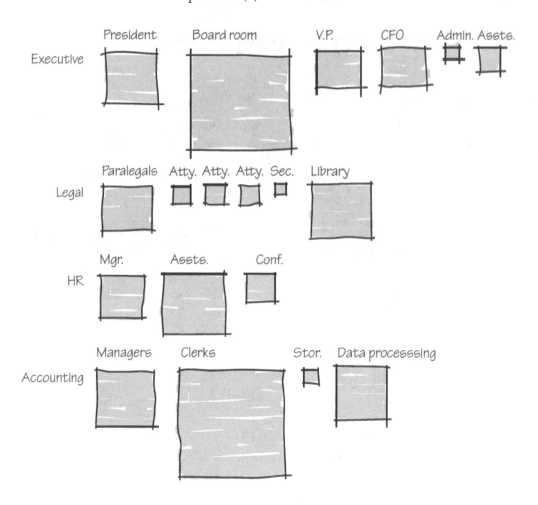

(A) function assignment

(B) block diagram

(C) departmental grouping

(D) area diagram

29. The primary advantage of an oblique drawing is that

(A) it shows the most realistic view of an object

(B) all three axes are drawn at the same scale

(C) existing orthographic drawings can be used as a starting point

(D) it shows foreshortened lines and planes accurately

30. What is the best source an interior designer could use to research the flammability and VOC ratings of several sofas the designer was considering specifying for a client?

(A) BIFMA standards

(B) each manufacturer's local representative

(C) the internet

(D) local showrooms that sell the sofas

31. What is the drawing shown most likely used for?

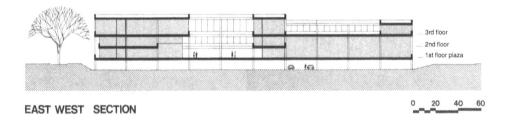

EAST WEST SECTION

0   20   40   60

(A)   as a starting point for design development

(B)   as a basis for construction documents

(C)   for the further development of a preliminary stacking diagram

(D)   to show the client a conceptual approach to a design

32. It is essential that sample boards include

(A)   color photographs of the furniture

(B)   a floor plan showing where each item will be used

(C)   actual samples of the materials

(D)   manufacturers' product data sheets

33. A designer is developing a large, multilevel retail space with a variety of finishes, lighting, and fixture types. How can the designer BEST communicate the design to the client if cost is not a factor?

(A)   draw several quick sketches of the space from different points of view

(B)   make a large-scale model with representations of the finishes applied

(C)   color a detailed perspective rendering as accurately as possible

(D)   commission a fully rendered 3-D computer model that can show a "fly-through"

34. What characterizes an isometric drawing?

(A)   All axes are drawn to the same scale.

(B)   A three-dimensional view can easily be created by tilting a floor plan and extending vertical lines.

(C)   Lines of projection are perpendicular to the picture plane.

(D)   The view shows a cut approximately 5 ft (1525 mm) above the floor.

35. During programming, what would the diagram shown be used for?

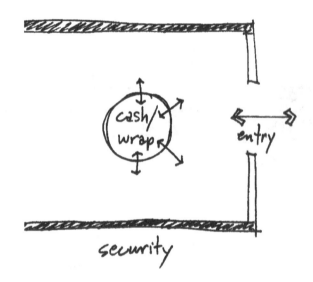

(A) recording notes from a client design meeting

(B) showing an analysis of one of the facts of the program

(C) exploring and presenting alternatives for design concepts

(D) presenting part of a summary of a programmatic concept

36. A designer has developed a new workstation layout for a large corporate client. The workstation is unlike anything the client has used previously. The designer could BEST communicate the design and functionality of the workstation by

(A) developing large-scale plan views with details and large-scale elevations

(B) having a full-scale mockup built that includes the actual workstation furniture being used

(C) rendering a detailed perspective drawing with accompanying finish and material samples

(D) commissioning a fully rendered, three-dimensional computer model that shows a "fly-through"

37. Which of these diagrams would be most appropriate for the planning of a small shopping mall?

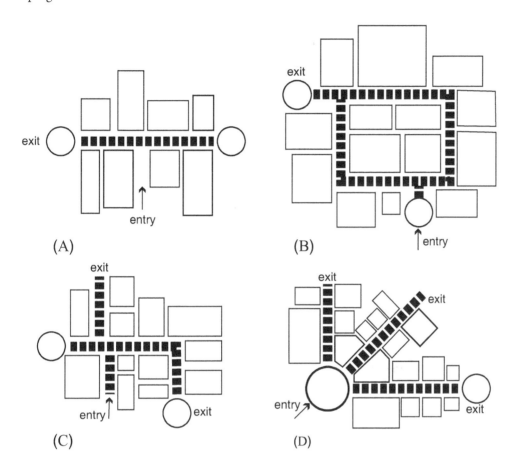

(A)

(B)

(C)

(D)

❹ LIFE SAFETY AND UNIVERSAL DESIGN

38. When coordinating the location of emergency warning systems consisting of audio and visual alarms as part of the reflected ceiling layout, the interior designer must coordinate with the

(A) electrical contractor

(B) electrical engineer

(C) fire protection engineer

(D) mechanical engineer

39. Which of the following pairs of building code requirements is MOST critical for the interior designer to know before starting the preliminary space planning?

(A) occupancy group and total floor area

(B) number of exits and maximum distance to exits

(C) allowable length of dead-end corridors and glazing requirements

(D) occupant load and corridor construction requirements

40. A clothing store located on the ground floor contains 15,000 ft² (1394 m²) of retail area, a 2000 ft² (186 m²) space for fashion shows for a seated audience with small cocktail tables, and a 3000 ft² (279 m²) stock room. Using the table shown, determine the total occupant load.

Occupancy Load Table

function of space	floor area in ft² (m²) per occupant
accessory storage areas, mechanical equipment rooms	300 (27.9) gross
assembly without fixed seats:	
concentrated (chairs only—not fixed)	7 (0.7) net
standing space	5 (0.5) net
unconcentrated (tables and chairs)	15 (1.4) net
business areas	100 (9.3) gross
education	
classroom area	20 (1.9) net
shops and other vocational room areas	50 (4.6) net
exercise rooms	50 (4.6) gross
kitchens, commercial	200 (18.6) gross
mercantile	
sales areas	60 (5.6) gross
storage, stock, shipping areas	300 (27.9) gross

(A) 394 occupants

(B) 434 occupants

(C) 546 occupants

(D) 660 occupants

41. A designer has calculated the occupant load of a large, sprinklered hotel ballroom, and has determined that three exits are required from the space. The diagonal distance of the room is 160 ft (14.9 m). According to the *International Building Code* (IBC), two of the exits must be separated by at least one-third of the diagonal distance of the room. Where does the code require the third exit to be located?

(A) a reasonable distance from the others

(B) a minimum of 80 ft (7.4 m) from the first two

(C) as determined by the building official

(D) at least one-half the diagonal distance from the first two

42. Which of the following partition wall assemblies would be the least expensive to provide a 1-hour fire rating in a Type V-A building?

(A) one layer of ⅝ in (16 mm) Type X gypsum board on each side of wood studs

(B) one layer of ⅝ in (16 mm) Type X gypsum board on each side of metal studs

(C) two layers of ½ in (13 mm) gypsum board on each side of metal studs

(D) two layers of ⅝ in (16 mm) Type X gypsum board on each side of wood studs

43. In starting a design project in a multi-use building, what information would an interior designer need to determine?

(A) construction type, adjacent occupancies, and sprinkler condition

(B) construction type, fire-zone classification, and accessibility requirements

(C) adjacent occupancies, sprinkler condition, and fire-zone classification

(D) adjacent occupancies, fire-zone classification, and accessibility requirements

44. A designer is developing a space plan for a full floor tenant in a high-rise building. The designer needs to know which of the following to determine the maximum travel distance allowed by the IBC?

(A) construction type and height of the building

(B) occupancy classification and whether the design involves an exit or exit access

(C) occupancy classification and whether the building is sprinklered

(D) construction type and whether the building is sprinklered

45. Which of the following are correct statements about corridors? (Choose the three that apply.)

(A) Corridors are part of the exit access.

(B) Corridors are part of the exit.

(C) Corridors must be used exclusively for egress.

(D) Corridor construction must be fire rated.

(E) Corridors are included in calculating travel distance.

(F) Corridors must never have dead ends.

46. An occupant load calculation has shown that an office suite requires a total of 71 in (1804 mm) of egress width and two exit access doors. In order to meet all *International Building Code* (IBC) and accessibility requirements, what are the minimum door widths that should be used?

(A) one 36 in door and one 42 in door (914 mm and 1067 mm)

(B) one 38 in door and one 34 in door (965 mm and 864 mm)

(C) one 36 in door and one 44 in door (914 mm and 1118 mm)

(D) two 36 in (914 mm) doors

47. When visiting a job site, the interior designer notices that a handrail appears to be out of place. When measuring it, the designer finds the top of the handrail to be 39½ in (1003 mm) above the nosing. In what direction and how far should the designer tell the contractor to move the handrail?

(A) up by ½ in (13 mm)

(B) down by 1½ in (38 mm)

(C) down by 3½ in (89 mm)

(D) down by 6 in (152 mm)

48. In which building type are fire-resistive construction requirements likely to be LEAST restrictive?

(A) Type I

(B) Type II

(C) Type III

(D) Type IV

49. Which of the following is the BEST choice for safety glazing in a hazardous location?

(A) tempered or laminated glass

(B) tempered or wired glass

(C) heat-strengthened glass or wired glass

(D) laminated glass or wired glass

50. In a fully sprinklered office building, how many sprinklers would be required in a room measuring 20 ft × 25 ft (6100 mm × 7620 mm)?

(A) 2 sprinklers

(B) 3 sprinklers

(C) 4 sprinklers

(D) 6 sprinklers

51. The two MOST important factors in determining the number of exits required for a particular room or space are the

(A) occupancy and the distance from the room exit to the building exit

(B) exit widths and the common path of egress travel

(C) occupant load and the building size

(D) occupancy and the occupant load

52. The three parts of a means of egress include the

(A) public way, exit, and exit access

(B) public way, exit access, and corridor

(C) exit access, exit, and exit discharge

(D) exit, exit enclosure, and exit discharge

53. Exits are ALWAYS

(A) protected by fire-resistance-rated construction

(B) limited in length

(C) constructed as either corridors or stairways

(D) required to have a 2-hour rating

54. Which of the following are the two main factors used to determine whether a space must have more than one exit?

(A) travel distance and exit width

(B) occupant load and occupancy

(C) travel distance and occupant load

(D) exit width and occupancy

55. When doing design work for remodeling toilet rooms to make them accessible, the designer finds that it is impossible to provide adequate clearance on one side of a door. What is the BEST course of action?

(A) Propose to the client that walls be demolished and replanned to provide the necessary clearances.

(B) Apply to the building department for a variance because of the remodeling problem.

(C) Specify a power-assisted door opener that meets accessibility standards and incorporate this into the design.

(D) Suggest that a unisex toilet be built nearby that complies with all accessibility requirements.

56. Which type of sink is BEST for barrier-free design?

(A) vanity

(B) pedestal

(C) wall hung

(D) free standing

57. The flame-spread rating of wood panel wainscoting must be

(A) a minimum of class A

(B) class B if the wainscoting takes up more than 10% of the wall area

(C) nothing, because it is not regulated

(D) based on location and occupancy

58. Refer to the illustration, which shows a reflected ceiling plan for an office space (do not use the ceiling grid as a scale). What is the maximum spacing of the sprinkler heads indicated by A and B, in accordance with National Fire Protection Association (NFPA) 13 for light hazard occupancies?

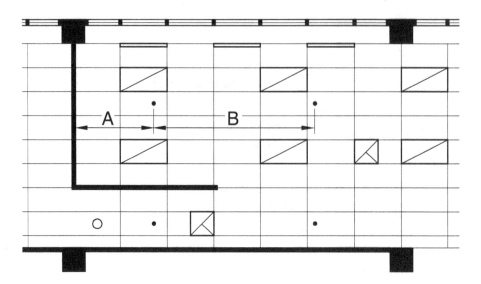

(A) A = 4 ft, B = 8 ft (1220 mm, 2440 mm)

(B) A = 5½ ft, B = 10 ft (1676 mm, 3048 mm)

(C) A = 7½ ft, B = 15 ft (2286 mm, 4572 mm)

(D) A = 10 ft, B = 17½ ft (3048 mm, 5334 mm)

59. An interior designer has received a construction cost estimate for an acoustical ceiling system. The area of the ceiling is 15,000 ft² (1394 m²). The estimate is $6000 over the budget. The owner requests that the currently specified 2 ft × 2 ft (610 mm × 610 mm) grid with tegular tiles be replaced with a less expensive system while maintaining acoustical qualities and a similar aesthetic. The contractor has provided pricing for alternative ceiling systems as shown in the matrix.

ceiling system type	quantity (ft² (m²))	unit cost ($/ft²)
tegular tile in 2 ft × 2 ft (610 mm × 610 mm) 9/16 in grid	15,000 (1394)	5.00
standard tile in 2 ft × 2 ft (610 mm × 610 mm) narrow grid	15,000 (1394)	4.80
standard tile in 2 ft × 2 ft (610 mm × 610 mm) standard T-bar	15,000 (1394)	4.40
drywall with level 4 finish	15,000 (1394)	4.20
standard tile in 2 ft × 4 ft (610 mm × 1220 mm) narrow grid	15,000 (1394)	3.20

Based on this pricing information and knowledge of the acoustical properties of each of these types of assemblies, which alternate system should the interior designer recommend to the client?

(A) drywall with level 4 finish

(B) standard tile in 2 ft × 2 ft (610 mm × 610 mm) narrow grid

(C) standard tile in 2 ft × 2 ft (610 mm × 610 mm) standard T-bar

(D) standard tile in 2 ft × 4 ft (610 mm × 1220 mm) narrow grid

60. An interior designer is looking for independent, third-party information specifically about a carpet's volatile organic compound (VOC) emissions. The BEST source would be the

(A) Green Label Plus program

(B) *GreenSpec Directory*

(C) Greenguard Environmental Institute

(D) U.S. Green Building Council

61. How can a drapery treatment be BEST changed to minimize its hazard during a fire?

(A) Shorten the length of the fabric.

(B) Use an open-weave fabric.

(C) Increase the amount of fabric.

(D) Use a composite fabric.

62. Which of the following statements is true about seismic restraint for suspended acoustical ceilings in seismic design categories D, E, and F as defined in the *International Building Code* (IBC)?

(A) All ceiling-high partitions must be braced independently from the grid.

(B) After determining the appropriate seismic design category, the interior designer can follow industry-standard detailing.

(C) Main runners must be securely attached to the ceiling angles on opposite sides of a room.

(D) Rigid compression struts are required at the grid intersections every 96 in (2.44 m) on center.

❺ INTERIOR BUILDING MATERIALS AND FINISHES

63. Which test is MOST frequently used to evaluate carpet in the United States?

(A) flooring radiant panel test

(B) Steiner tunnel test

(C) methenamine pill test

(D) methods of fire tests of building construction and materials

64. In developing a signage system for a health care clinic, the designer decides that the room identification signs should be mounted perpendicular to the wall near the door to each room. Which of the following are of greatest concern in the design work? (Choose the four that apply.)

(A)   the color of the lettering and its background

(B)   that the amount the Braille lettering is raised above the surface

(C)   whether or not the width of the accessible route is reduced

(D)   the mounting height to the center of the sign

(E)   the use of the standard ADA font

(F)   whether or not the lettering is uppercase

65. What type of system would be MOST appropriate in a large commercial remodeling project where a decorative acoustical ceiling and plenum access are required?

(A)   integrated

(B)   linear metal strip

(C)   gypsum wallboard

(D)   concealed spline

66. What is the purpose of construction element A in the following diagram of a wood floor?

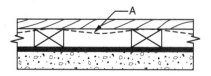

(A)   to minimize squeaking

(B)   to prevent chemicals from the subfloor from contaminating the wood

(C)   to act as a vapor barrier

(D)   to provide added resiliency

67. An interior designer has been retained for a building project that is currently being planned by an architect. On the second floor of the building, slate flooring over a concrete subfloor is being used. What type of installation should ideally be designed for?

(A)   a thick-set application using a cleavage membrane

(B)   a bonded thick-set installation

(C)   a $^1/_2$ in (12 mm) layer of mortar with the stone dry-set on top

(D)   a standard thin-set installation

68. A 216 pitch carpet has

(A)   a pile height that is almost $^1/_4$ in (6 mm) high

(B)   8 surface yarns per inch (25 mm)

(C)   an equivalent gauge of $^1/_6$

(D)   a commercial-grade stitch rate

69. An interior designer is developing plans for the ceiling in a 25,000 ft² (2323 m²) corporate office. The program calls for the office space to consist of 70% closed offices and rooms and 30% open office space. The program has also specified that the operation of the company changes frequently, requiring rearrangement of personnel teams and project organizations. Assuming a relocatable partition system is used, which type of ceiling system should the interior designer recommend to the client?

(A) custom track system

(B) 60 in (1524 mm) lay-in acoustical grid

(C) integrated ceiling system

(D) narrow bar exposed T-bar system

70. A window covering that is made from fabric and is generally not intended to be opened is called

(A) a curtain

(B) an Austrian shade

(C) a vertical blind

(D) drapery

71. When specifying a specialty flooring material, the interior designer can obtain unbiased information on the hazards of a cleaning agent required for maintenance from the

(A) cleaning agent manufacturer

(B) Environmental Protection Agency (EPA)

(C) flooring manufacturer

(D) safety data sheet

72. What type of wall treatment would be appropriate for an office waiting room where durability and low cost are required?

(A) fabric wallcovering

(B) thin stone tiles

(C) vinyl wallcovering

(D) wood veneer paneling

73. Information concerning limitations on the use of a product can BEST be obtained from the

(A) building code official who inspects the product

(B) specialty contractor who installs the product

(C) manufacturer who makes the product

(D) trade association representing the product type

74. What type of resilient flooring would be the BEST choice for a commercial kitchen?

(A) $^{1}/_{8}$ in (3 mm) commercial-grade vinyl tile

(B)   sheet vinyl

(C)   heavy-duty cork flooring

(D)   sheet rubber

75. In the illustration shown, the purpose of the device in the vertical partition section is to

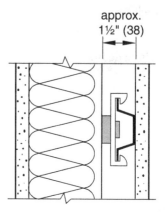

approx.
1½" (38)

(A)   minimize reverberation

(B)   increase the sound absorption average (SAA)

(C)   reduce sound transmission

(D)   decrease potential impact noise

❻ TECHNICAL SPECIFICATIONS FOR FURNITURE, FIXTURES, & EQUIPMENT AND LIGHTING

76. What is the MOST important criterion for lighting a fabric showroom?

(A)   visual comfort probability

(B)   color rendering index

(C)   coefficient of utilization

(D)   apparent color temperature rating

77. Which type of lighting would BEST enhance the appearance of a rough, plastered wall?

(A)   fluorescent cove uplighting on all four sides of the room

(B)   decorative chandeliers near the wall

(C)   track lighting near the center of the room, aimed at the wall

(D)   recessed incandescents close to the wall

78. Which method of veneer cut results in the straightest grain possible from MOST species of trees?

- (A) half-round slicing
- (B) quarter slicing
- (C) flat slicing
- (D) rotary slicing

79. When specifying the method by which two veneer pieces are to be applied, the MOST pleasing result is usually obtained with a

- (A) balance match
- (B) book match
- (C) center match
- (D) slip match

80. The most naturally fire-resistant untreated fabric is

- (A) acrylic
- (B) cotton
- (C) nylon
- (D) wool

81. What fabric would have the BEST appearance for the longest time when used in theater seating?

- (A) vinyl
- (B) wool-nylon blend
- (C) acrylic-acetate blend
- (D) cotton-rayon blend

82. An interior designer is selecting luminaires and lamp sources to illuminate the waiting area of a medical clinic for which the furniture and finishes have been selected. In order to maintain the most accurate color rendition of the furniture and finishes, what is the best approach for selecting the lamps?

- (A) Select those with the highest color rendering index (CRI).
- (B) Analyze the correlated color temperature (CCT) of the lamps.
- (C) Review the spectral energy distribution curves.
- (D) View the samples under each lamp being considered.

83. Important criteria for designing a lighting cove would include which of the following? (Choose the four that apply.)

(A)   cost

(B)   design intent

(C)   ergonomics

(D)   aesthetics

(E)   support framing

(F)   lighting level

84.   Which pair of performance tests should be specified for a custom-blended fabric that will be used in a recreation center's reception area?

(A)   vertical ignition and Fade-Ometer

(B)   Wyzenbeek and Fade-Ometer

(C)   Taber and Wyzenbeek

(D)   indentation load deflection and Taber

85.   Which of the following items does NFPA 701 relate to?

(A)   wallcoverings

(B)   fabrics

(C)   draperies

(D)   floor coverings

86.   Which of the following must have AT LEAST a Class III (or C) fire rating?

(A)   bookshelves

(B)   wainscoting

(C)   built-in base cabinets

(D)   door and window trim

87.   An interior designer has specified a single downlight to illuminate a pedestal directly below. If the downlight produces 1470 candlepower (cp) and is 7 ft above the pedestal, the illumination on the pedestal is _____ footcandles (fc). (Fill in the blank.)

88.   The BEST way to avoid fabric slippage over a cushion would be to specify

(A)   a heavy fabric pulled tightly over the cushion

(B)   a high-density foam cushion with an interliner

(C)   rounded corners with welts

(D)   channeling

89.   The model number and color of a piece of furniture would commonly be found on

(A)   the furniture plan

(B)   the furniture schedule only

(C)   the specifications only

(D)   either a furniture schedule or the specifications

90. When considering the safety of smooth flooring materials, the interior designer should

    (A)   specify materials with a rough finish

    (B)   require that the dynamic coefficient of friction have a value of 0.42 or greater

    (C)   consider the values given by the DCOF AcuTest as well as other variables

    (D)   use the coefficient of friction values and recommendations of ASTM C1028

91. When reviewing flooring materials to determine which options meet life safety and accessibility standards for slip resistance, the interior designer should

    (A)   have the material tested

    (B)   review the coefficient of friction (COF)

    (C)   verify requirements of the Americans with Disabilities Act (ADA)

    (D)   study pertinent ASTM International standards

92. Which of the following normally shows the locations of exit signs?

    (A)   floor plan

    (B)   reflected ceiling plan

    (C)   life safety plan

    (D)   fire protection plan

93. Which of the following terms represents the efficiency of a luminaire in distributing lamp light to room surfaces?

    (A)   coefficient of utilization

    (B)   lamp lumen depreciation factor

    (C)   lamp luminance

    (D)   luminaire efficacy

94. Surface-mounted luminaires are MOST often used for which of the following reasons?

    (A)   Some side and uplighting is desired.

    (B)   There is not enough space above the ceiling.

    (C)   They are easier and less expensive to install.

    (D)   They are used as a design feature.

❼ CONSTRUCTION DRAWINGS, SCHEDULES, AND SPECIFICATIONS

95. The cover sheet on a set of interior design construction drawings typically includes which of the following? (Choose the four that apply.)

(A) building department data

(B) client's name and address

(C) index to drawings

(D) small-scale reference floor plan

(E) symbols used on the drawings

(F) zoning department information

96. Composite wood veneers can be used

(A) to improve the appearance of book matching

(B) as a substitute for HPDL

(C) as a "green" alternate to standard wood veneers

(D) to increase the yield of veneer from a log

97. An interior designer is preparing drawings for a tenant build-out. Which of the following items are required by the *International Building Code* (IBC) when submitting for a building permit? (Choose the four that apply.)

(A) finish schedule or finish plan

(B) architectural millwork details

(C) all portions of the means of egress

(D) custom furniture drawings

(E) mechanical drawings

(F) plan of interior space relative to entire floor or building

98. What should be called out on cabinet drawings to ensure the BEST fit and appearance next to existing construction?

(A) reveals around all edges

(B) spacers at cabinet backs

(C) scribe pieces at cabinet edges

(D) blocking, where necessary

99. For the most durable wood finish, which of the following finish types should be specified?

(A) lacquer

(B) penetrating oil

(C) polyurethane

(D) varnish

100. Furniture plans for commercial projects typically include which of the following? (Choose the four that apply.)

(A)   code number for each piece of furniture

(B)   computers

(C)   desk lamp location

(D)   furniture location

(E)   partitions

(F)   telephone and data outlets

101. Specifications can be made MOST concise by

(A)   using reference standard specifications

(B)   avoiding the use of such words as "a," "the," and "all"

(C)   using phrases instead of complete sentences

(D)   using descriptive specifications

102. The drawing shown in the illustration is an example of a(n)

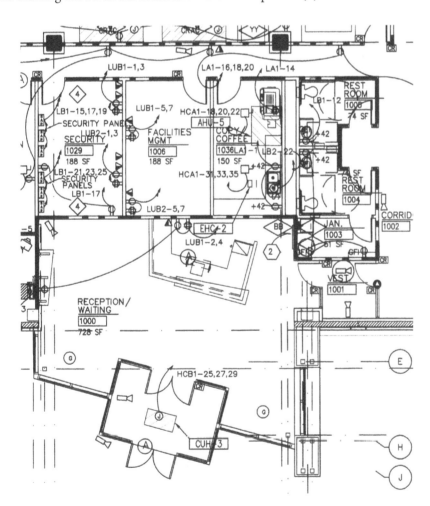

(A)   electrical plan

(B)   power plan

(C)   telephone/electrical plan

(D)   lighting plan

103. Division 05 of the MasterFormat system includes which of the following?

(A)   doors

(B)   wall finishes

(C)   ornamental metal

(D)   architectural woodwork

104. Which of the following interior design services is normally performed during a project's contract documents phase?

(A)   coordinating the consultant contracts

(B)   performing a code review

(C)   preparing furniture drawings

(D)   reviewing shop drawings

105. Which of the following generally include the MOST detailed information about doors? (Choose the four that apply.)

(A)   schedules

(B)   floor plans

(C)   enlarged floor plans

(D)   room elevations

(E)   specifications

(F)   shop drawings

106. An interior designer would minimize potential conflicts in the contract documents by doing which of the following? (Choose the four that apply.)

(A)   showing dimensions on only the drawings, not in the specifications

(B)   having someone who has not worked on the project check the drawings before they are issued

(C)   writing the project specifications after the drawings are completed

(D)   ensuring that terminology in the specifications matches the drawings' terminology

(E)   developing a new drawing sheet organization method to match the needs of each project

(F)   using a master specification

107. Window treatments should be specified in which MasterFormat division?

    (A)   08

    (B)   09

    (C)   10

    (D)   12

108. In the drawing shown, where else would the capital letters under each elevation be found?

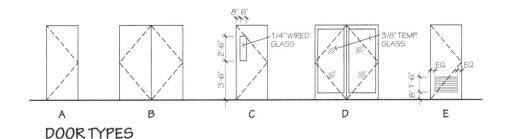

DOOR TYPES

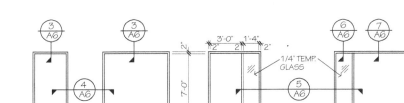

FRAME TYPES

    (A)   with the frame details

    (B)   in the specifications

    (C)   on the door schedule

    (D)   on the hardware schedule

109. The full extent of slab-to-slab partitions on a project is best shown on the

    (A)   reflected ceiling plan

    (B)   interior elevations

    (C)   wall section details

    (D)   finish plan

110. Dimensions on interior design floor plans are commonly drawn from the

    (A)   centerlines of partitions

    (B)   finish faces of partitions

    (C)   face of studs or structural walls

    (D)   centerlines of structural walls and finish faces of partitions

111. Drawings for a single floor in a high-rise building containing commercial office spaces would MOST likely use what form of sheet notation?

(A) 1, 2, 3, 4, and so on

(B) A1, A2, A3, A4, and so on

(C) A1.1, A1.2, A2.1, A2.2, and so on

(D) A23.1, A23.2, A23.3, A23.4, and so on

112. An interior designer has drawn a floor plan of a large office space to a scale of ⅛ in = 1 ft 0 in (1:100) and determines that an enlarged floor plan of the toilet rooms needs to be included. What information should be shown on the enlarged floor plan that is not shown on the small-scale plans? (Choose the four that apply.)

(A) room names and numbers

(B) dimensions to centerlines of fixtures

(C) door swings of toilet partitions

(D) dimensions to walls within the toilet rooms

(E) dimensions of toilet partitions

(F) toilet accessories with a key to a schedule

113. An interior designer is developing a floor plan for a new tenant in an existing office space and will reuse a number of existing partitions to meet LEED reusability requirements. What notation should the interior designer use on the demolition plan to clearly distinguish partitions to be removed from partitions to be reused?

(A) solid lines for partitions being removed and dashed lines for partitions being reused

(B) solid lines for partitions being removed and solid black fill for partitions being reused

(C) dashed lines for partitions being removed and solid lines for partitions being reused

(D) dashed lines for partitions being reused and solid black fill for partitions being removed

114. Which of the following information about gypsum wallboard partitions should be part of a project's specifications, not its drawings?

(A) edge treatment

(B) fastener spacing

(C) stud depth

(D) wallboard thickness

115. Which of the following schedules are MOST likely to be found on a set of interior design drawings? (Choose the four that apply.)

- (A) luminaire schedule
- (B) window schedule
- (C) door schedule
- (D) equipment schedule
- (E) millwork schedule
- (F) toilet accessory schedule

116. What is illustrated in the following partial drawing?

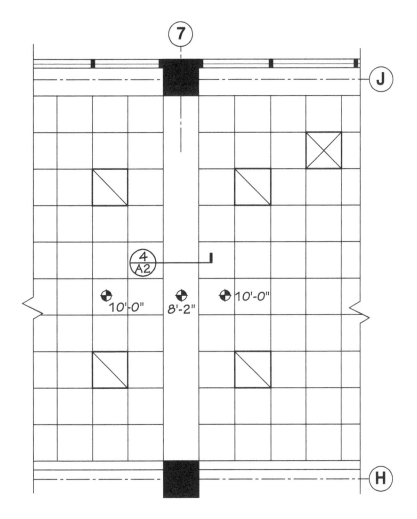

- (A) floor finish plan
- (B) floor plan
- (C) lighting plan
- (D) reflected ceiling plan

117. On a remodeling project with new construction, including partitions, a demolition plan is necessary when

(A)   there is a complex mix of items to be removed and new construction

(B)   the authority having jurisdiction (AHJ) requires a separate demolition plan

(C)   the sustainability plan requires recycling and reuse of removed items

(D)   the contractor requests it in order to speed construction and avoid mistakes

118. The drawing shown occurs at the exterior wall of a high-rise building. The purpose of this detail is to

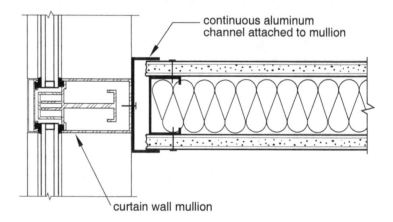

continuous aluminum channel attached to mullion

curtain wall mullion

(A)   allow for installation of a modular partition

(B)   provide for lateral movement of the building

(C)   provide for a finished end of the partition

(D)   give a tight seal to limit sound transmission

119. Which of the following symbols should be used to indicate that an interior glazing jamb shown on a floor plan is detailed on another drawing sheet?

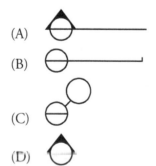

(A)

(B)

(C)

(D)

❽ PROFESSIONAL DEVELOPMENT AND ETHICS

120. For a member of the American Society of Interior Designers (ASID), which action is a clear violation of ASID Code of Ethics?

(A) allowing the client to pay the designer with a part interest in the project instead of money

(B) not disclosing that the interior designer has a financial interest in the building where the client's project will be located

(C) as an employer, giving permission to an employee leaving the firm to take drawings on projects the employee worked on

(D) sharing nonproprietary information about a project type with another allied professional

121. An interior designer has been hired by a client to design an office space. The client tells the designer to use discount chairs in order to save money. The designer initially agrees that the style and comfort level of the chairs will be compatible with the other furniture the designer will be selecting. On further investigation, however, the designer discovers that the chairs do not meet required VOC limits or flammability standards. What should the designer do?

(A) give the client documentation about the VOC and flammability standards, and tell the client that the designer cannot incorporate the chairs in the designs but will look for substitutes

(B) suggest that the client try to find other chairs from the same discount source that will meet the VOC and flammability standards

(C) accept use of the chairs

(D) find substitute chairs as close as possible to the client's in cost but that meet the VOC and flammability standards

122. Which of the following major areas is included in the ASID Code of Ethics but not in the IIDA Code of Ethics?

(A) responsibility to the public

(B) responsibility to the profession

(C) responsibility to the employer

(D) responsibility to other interior designers and colleagues

123. Interior designers can continue to develop their knowledge, serve their community, and enhance their professional development by

(A) participating in trade association work

(B) volunteering in the community

(C) serving on design review boards

(D) teaching or mentoring young professionals

124. The American Society of Interior Designers (ASID) is an example of a

    (A)   constituency-based organization

    (B)   cause-based organization

    (C)   knowledge-based organization

    (D)   combination of constituency-based, cause-based, and knowledge-based organization

125. What are some of the advantages of continuing education for the interior designer? (Choose the four that apply.)

    (A)   It is a way to advance the designer's career.

    (B)   It is a way to keep up to date with changes in the profession.

    (C)   It is required by all states and Canadian provinces.

    (D)   It is required for membership in many professional organizations.

    (E)   It ensures all designers have a comparable level of knowledge.

    (F)   It encourages professional organizations to develop learning opportunities.

MOCK EXAM ANSWERS

Once you have completed your mock exam, compare your answers to those on the answer key that follows. The explanations to these answers begin on the page following the answer key.

❶ Programming and Site Analysis	❷ Relationship Between Human Behavior and the Designed Environment	❸ Design Communication Techniques	❹ Life Safety and Universal Design
1. A, D, E			
2. A		26. A	38. D
3. A, B, C, E		27. C	39. B
4. B	14. B	28. D	40. A
5. B	15. B	29. C	41. A
6. B	16. D	30. B	42. B
7. A	17. D	31. D	43. A
8. C	18. C	32. C	44. C
9. C	19. B	33. D	45. A, C, E
10. B	20. C	34. A	46. A
11. D	21. B	35. C	47. C
12. C	22. A	36. B	48. D
13. D	23. D	37. A	49. A
	24. B, C, E, F		50. C
	25. A		51. D
			52. C
			53. A
			54. B
			55. C
			56. C
			57. D
			58. C
			59. C
			60. A
			61. A
			62. A

❺ Interior Building Materials and Finishes

63. C
64. B, C, D, F
65. D
66. C
67. A
68. B
69. C
70. A
71. D
72. C
73. C
74. B
75. C

❻ Technical Specifications for Funiture, Fixtures, & Equipment and Lighting

76. B
77. D
78. B
79. B
80. D
81. B
82. D
83. A, B, D, F
84. B
85. C
86. B
87. 30 fc
88. D
89. D
90. C
91. B
92. B
93. A
94. B

❼ Construction Drawings, Schedules, and Specifications

95. A, B, C, E
96. C
97. A, C, E, F
98. C
99. C
100. A, D, E, F
101. A
102. B
103. C
104. C
105. A, B, E, F
106. A, B, D, F
107. D
108. C
109. A
110. B
111. D
112. B, D, E, F
113. C
114. B
115. A, C, D, E
116. D
117. A
118. B
119. C

❽ Professional Development and Ethics

120. B
121. A
122. C
123. D
124. D
125. A, B, D, E

❶ PROGRAMMING AND SITE ANALYSIS

1. *The answer is A, D, and E.* An adjacency matrix, or affinity matrix, is a way of graphically representing which spaces should be adjacent to one another. This simple diagram is read by following the lines representing the spaces, to the box at which they meet. If there is a closed (black) dot in the box, the rooms should be adjacent to one another. If the dot is open (white), the spaces have some relationship but need not be adjacent. Where the box is empty, there is no direct or indirect adjacency requirement that needs to be met.

2. *The answer is A.* There are usually more design concepts than there are programmatic concepts. A programmatic concept is a performance requirement, not the other way around. Design concepts are based on and generated after programmatic concepts, not before.

3. *The answer is A, B, C, and E.* Whether the office space is open plan, closed plan, or some combination of the two depends on the specific requirements of the program; the type of plan employed is a result of the analysis of the planning criteria. Adjacencies, daylighting, egress paths and requirements, and the desired efficiency factor are necessary for function, sustainability, safety, and economy, so they are generally critical planning concerns. While column locations can influence how partitions and other aspects of the plan are laid out, they can usually be accommodated and are not a critical concern.

4. *The answer is B.* Option B is a bubble diagram. These diagrams are often used to indicate required adjacencies and priorities among relationships. Although a bubble diagram is often derived from the matrix chart shown in option A, the bubble diagram is better for showing relationships just before space planning. The relative sizes and positions of the bubbles indicate spatial relationships and sizes of the various spaces needed.

   Option C is a flow diagram, as indicated by the arrows. The flow diagram is used as a scheduling chart or to show a flow of materials or another kind of process from one point to another. Option D is a block diagram, which is used in the first stage of space planning and is based on an adjacency diagram or bubble diagram. It is not the correct answer because the question asks which diagram will be best just before the start of space planning.

5. *The answer is B.* Although all the options would influence the dining area's space plan, the actual building dimensions (which include the existing structural columns and walls) would determine whether the proposed dining area would even fit within the space available. This would be the most important element to determine well before thinking about plumbing, millwork, or lighting fixtures.

6. *The answer is B.* The rentable area is calculated by multiplying the usable area by the rentable-usable ratio. The usable area includes the net assignable area plus allowance for circulation, so no increase for this is required.

7. *The answer is A.* There are three basic types of required adjacencies: those that require person-to-person contacts, those that require the transfer of objects, and those that require an electronic transfer of information. When person-to-person contact is required, two or more spaces must be physically located next to each other. When object transfer is required, the spaces need not be adjacent if the objects can be transported without one person physically handing something to another person. Electronic transfers can be done over any distance.

8. *The answer is C.* Client interviews are one of the best ways to gather valuable information about the needs and wants of a given population. Interviews combine targeted question-and-answer sessions with observation and extemporaneous exploration of issues.

    Observation alone only shows what currently exists and not what may be needed. Questionnaires can be useful, but people only respond to specific questions, and it is difficult to ensure the questionnaires are completed accurately. Benchmarks are average data about a given topic, such as the typical area of an office, and are not an information-gathering technique.

9. *The answer is C.* It is very likely that information concerning the other three matters would be available from a good, complete set of construction drawings. A field survey would be most necessary to determine what sources of noise exist and their magnitudes.

10. *The answer is B.* The most immediate concerns for an interior designer doing a residential addition project are the required zoning setbacks and the capacities of the sewer system. Neighborhood character, traffic, and street characteristics, though important in other ways, are not critical issues affecting the design.

11. *The answer is D.* Understanding a client's sustainability goals is important so that the designer can assist the owner in finding and choosing a project site that supports these goals. For example, a building in a crowded urban area will have limited natural light. If using natural light is one of the client's goals, then the interior designer may suggest the client look at another building or location where natural light is more available.

12. *The answer is C.* A sprinkler system is governed by local building codes and affects many aspects of planning, exiting, materials use, and finishes. The lack of a sprinkler system can affect egress layout, finishes, and requirements for fire-rated construction, all in ways that would increase design costs and make specific design features necessary.

While each of the other three factors is important, the location of exits would affect the design cost less than the lack of a sprinkler system, and neither the limited views and daylight nor the remote electrical closet would affect the design cost significantly.

13. *The answer is D.* The book *Problem Seeking* states that establishing goals is the critical first step in the five-step process because it sets the direction for the other four steps, which are collecting and analyzing facts, uncovering and testing concepts, determining needs, and stating the problem.

❷ RELATIONSHIP BETWEEN HUMAN BEHAVIOR AND THE DESIGNED ENVIRONMENT

14. *The answer is B.* Territoriality is the human need to lay claim to the space one occupies. The two sets of identical furnishings, organized around an imaginary (but perceived) line, divide the dormitory room into two equal territories. Each roommate could then personalize one of the territories.

15. *The answer is B.* To justify using bright colors in an elderly care facility, the interior designer could refer to evidence from research that suggests that bright colors have a positive effect on the health and well-being of the elderly. Using evidence from research to support a design decision is an example of evidence-based design. Design theory, Gestalt psychology, and historic precedent would not have much relevance to this particular design choice.

16. *The answer is D.* Religious beliefs and ceremony are strongly connected with the use of symbols; therefore, an interior designer should first take symbolism into account. While cultural attitudes, proxemics, and regionalism could also be incorporated into the design concept, symbolism has the strongest relevance.

17. *The answer is D.* Proxemics is the study of personal space needs and the application of that knowledge to actual space planning. Of the four options, determining the design of seating where people will be very close to each other is the situation where proxemics would be most helpful.

18. *The answer is C.* Typically, designers are influenced by regionalism, which is the idea that the design of a home should reflect the unique characteristics of its geographical region. This can be accomplished while still responding to the unique needs and spatial requirements of the client.

19. *The answer is B.* Manipulating scale through the physical placement of walls, ceilings, and other architectural elements is the strongest way to create the feeling of intimacy. The use of pattern, texture, and color, while important elements in setting a mood, will have little effect if the physical size of the space is too great.

20. *The answer is C.* Warm colors tend to advance, and darker values tend to make objects look heavier. This makes a sofa with a warm hue and dark value (option C) the best choice, especially when the sofa can be contrasted with a much lighter background. A light-colored sofa contrasted with a much darker background (option B) is the next best choice; however, option C is the best choice to make the sofa appear heavier.

21. *The answer is B.* Highly saturated complementary colors reinforce each other, so the second combination would create the highest contrast and be the easiest to see for people of all ages. Option D could be the next best combination, depending on how the colors and white were used. For example, a sign with yellow lettering on a white background would be very difficult to see.

22. *The answer is A.* Dark values tend to make surfaces seem closer, as do heavy textures. The two in combination would make the ceiling appear lower.

23. *The answer is D.* Maslow's conceptual model is based on an inherent hierarchy of needs, as shown in the figure. The hierarchy ranges from the most basic deficiency needs, such as the need for food, water, and minimal bodily comforts, to higher-level needs, such as the need for belonging, the need for aesthetic satisfaction, and the need for self-actualization. The ability to satisfy these needs can affect a person's activities and interactions with their environment.

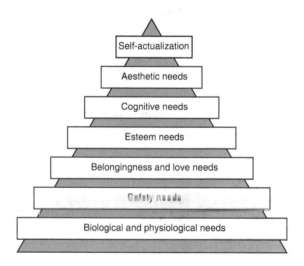

According to behavior setting theory, there are definable boundaries and objects in which a standing pattern of behavior occurs at a particular time. These patterns of behavior are useful for connecting human activity with the effects of the physical environment.

Proxemics describes how people use space as a specialized elaboration of culture. This theory also deals with issues such as spacing between people, territoriality, and the organization of space.

McClelland's theory states that every person has one of three main driving motivators: the need for achievement, the need for affiliation, or the need for power. These motivators are developed through learning and development rather than being inherent in a person's nature.

24. *The answer is B, C, E, and F.* Chairs and other seating, integration of bariatric seating with standard seating, equipment storage for things such as mobility devices and lift devices, and bedside amenities are all within the area of knowledge and responsibility of the interior designer.

Room size, which includes providing space for health care workers around a bed, and door sizes are aspects of the design that the architect is responsible for, not the interior designer.

25. *The answer is A.* Although all four options could emphasize the object, option A uses location, position, and lighting to focus attention on the item. Option C may be the next best choice, but depending on what the item is, making an oversized model may distort its image.

❸ DESIGN COMMUNICATION TECHNIQUES

26. *The answer is A.* The diagram shown is an adjacency block diagram. It shows both the desired adjacencies (like a bubble diagram) and the relative sizes of spaces (like an area diagram) in a simple block form. An adjacency block diagram helps the designer visualize how the various spaces must be organized, without ancillary spaces such as corridors, mechanical rooms, and the like.

The division of spaces in zones would already have been determined in the program. The maximum floor areas would be determined by the program listing. A stacking diagram would be a separate graphic and not necessarily related to this.

27. *The answer is C.* A perspective drawing gives the most realistic view of three-dimensional space on two-dimensional media. It will be effective and clear even if the client is not experienced in interpreting architectural drawings.

28. *The answer is D.*   The illustration is an example of an area diagram showing the relative square footage required for the various rooms or spaces. A block diagram shows rough areas of assignable space within the building floor plan and with their required adjacencies. Function assignments and departmental groupings are not names used in preliminary planning.

29. *The answer is C.*   An oblique drawing has one of its planes parallel to the picture plane, so an existing floor plan or elevation can be used as the starting point. The third dimension is then represented by project lines at any convenient angle.

Perspective is the most realistic view of an object. In an oblique drawing, one of the axes must be drawn at a different scale so the drawing does not look distorted. In an oblique view, foreshortened lines are still distorted.

30. *The answer is B.*   Manufacturers, dealers, and representatives are the most reliable sources of current information on specific products, including flammability and VOC (volatile organic compounds) ratings. However, while some manufacturer's web sites contain technical information on flammability and VOC ratings, it can be difficult to find, as most manufacturers are more interested in showing and selling their products than in providing technical information. Therefore, the best source of information is manufacturer's representative.

The standards of the Business and Institutional Furniture Manufacturers Association (BIFMA) simply give the requirements that a particular type of furniture must meet. Local showrooms can sometimes provide technical information, but even they may have to contact the manufacturer's local representative.

31. *The answer is D.*   The drawing shown is a schematic design developed to show the client a conceptual approach to a design.

It is not detailed enough to act as a starting point for design development because it lacks dimensions, material indications, and other design development information. It is also very preliminary and not suitable for giving guidance for the beginning of construction documents.

Stacking diagrams are used to record what spaces will be planned on each floor. These diagrams are not a basis for further development.

32. *The answer is C.*   Only an actual sample can accurately convey a material's finish, color, and texture. It can be helpful to include the other three items as well, but actual material samples are essential.

33. *The answer is D.*   When cost is not a factor, the designer can best communicate the design of a complex space by commissioning a fully rendered 3-D computer model that can show a "fly-through." With this capability, the model can show the variety of finishes, lighting, and fixture types on all levels of the large, multilevel retail space from different points of view. The other methods (i.e., sketches, large-scale models, and detailed perspective renderings) can also communicate designs to clients. They are less thorough than 3-D models, but may be preferable when cost is a factor.

34. *The answer is A.* An isometric drawing uses the same scale for all axes. Option B refers to a plan oblique drawing. Option C refers to an orthographic drawing. Option D refers to a floor plan.

35. *The answer is C.* This diagram is a sketch of a design concept as one possible alternative to satisfy a programmatic concept for the design of a retail store. In this example the programmatic concept might have been: Provide a medium level of security to protect against theft of merchandise without making the security methods obvious. This diagram represents one possible design concept that the designer could use to begin design on a cash/wrap station at the entry and exit point to the store. This way clerks could sell merchandise and also observe people coming and going. If this concept was accepted by the client, it could further be designed in any number of configurations, shapes, and materials.

It is unlikely that a drawing like this would be used as a note from a client meeting.

This illustration also does not show a "fact" of the program: a fact-based diagram would probably show an arrow with the number of people that coming in the shop daily. It is also not a programmatic concept as described above.

36. *The answer is B.* Although any of the options listed could help describe the design, a full-scale mockup is the most effective way to show how the workstation would truly look and function. The client could not only view the mockup, but actually sit and move about in it to test its layout and design.

37. *The answer is A.* Diagram A represents a single double-loaded corridor concept with possible entries at one end or in the middle of the mall. The circles could also represent anchor stores at either end of the mall. The anchor stores encourage shoppers to move from one end to the other, with the entry perpendicular to the corridor. Once shoppers are in the mall, they can see the end and know where they are. This arrangement also offers an opportunity for stores to have exterior exposure with windows, secondary entries, or back entries for deliveries.

Diagram B also offers a double-loaded arrangement, but it is difficult to be oriented and know where the end of the mall is. There is also no opportunity for the stores in the middle of the mall to have any exterior exposure. Any service to those stores would have to cross the pedestrian portion of the mall. The many branching corridors in diagram C will make orientation difficult. The arrangement in diagram D requires shoppers to go back and forth between the exits and the central entry space to reach all the shops.

❹ LIFE SAFETY AND UNIVERSAL DESIGN

38. *The answer is D.* The mechanical engineer is responsible for locating and specifying the alarm devices required. The interior designer is responsible for coordinating the location of the warning systems on the reflected ceiling plan within the parameters of the life safety and building codes.

Accessibility codes require that both visual and audible alarms be provided. Audible alarms must produce a sound that exceeds the prevailing sound level in the room or space by at least 15 dB. Visual alarms must be flashing lights that have a flashing frequency of about 1 cycle/sec. The electrical contractor, electrical engineer, and fire protection engineer are involved with these warning systems only to the extent that they provide connections between the electrical system and the alarm devices.

39. *The answer is B.* Although there are many building code requirements that the designer needs to know before starting to plan, of the options given, only the number of exits and the maximum distance to exits are critical for preliminary space layout. Option A is incorrect because neither the occupancy group nor the floor area helps to suggest how the space should be laid out. Option C is incorrect because glazing requirements are not a critical element. Option D is incorrect because the details of corridor construction are not needed at this stage; only the corridor locations are needed.

40. *The answer is A.* From the table, mercantile areas have an occupant load of 60 ft² (5.6 m²) per occupant. An assembly area without fixed seats of unconcentrated use has an occupant load of 15 ft² (1.4 m²). A stock room has an occupant load of 300 ft² (27.9 m²) per occupant. Therefore,

$$\text{mercantile} = \frac{15{,}000 \text{ ft}^2}{60 \frac{\text{ft}^2}{\text{occupant}}} = 250 \text{ occupants}$$

$$\text{assembly} = \frac{2000 \text{ ft}^2}{15 \frac{\text{ft}^2}{\text{occupant}}} = 133.33 \text{ occupants (134 occupants)}$$

$$\text{stock room} = \frac{3000 \text{ ft}^2}{300 \frac{\text{ft}^2}{\text{occupant}}} = 10 \text{ occupants}$$

total = 250 occupants + 134 occupants + 10 occupants = 394 occupants

41. *The answer is A.*   The IBC requires that when three or four exits are required, two of the exits must be placed at least one-half the diagonal distance of the space for nonsprinklered spaces, and at least one-third the diagonal distance for sprinklered spaces. The third exit must be arranged a reasonable distance from the other two, so that if one of those exits becomes blocked, the other two will remain available.

42. *The answer is B.*   The basic assembly for a 1-hour-rated partition uses ⅝ in (16 mm) Type X gypsum wallboard on both sides of either wood or metal studs. In a Type V-A building, either type of stud can be used. However, metal stud framing is typically less expensive than wood framing. In order to achieve the desired rating, the partition must be constructed in accordance with an approved UL detail using the same combination of products and installation methods that has been tested in a laboratory and proven to have the desired fire resistance rating.

Using wood studs with ⅝ in (16 mm) gypsum board on both sides of the wall would provide a 1-hour rating, but wood stud framing is typically more expensive than metal stud framing. Two layers of standard ½ in (13 mm) gypsum board on each side of the studs meets the requirements for a 1-hour partition even without being Type X, but it would cost more to install two layers than a single layer.

43. *The answer is A.*   This question implies that the design process cannot proceed without some basic data that the interior designer might not otherwise have about a building. The most important pieces of information are construction type, adjacent occupancies, and sprinkler condition. Construction type could affect the maximum area of the client's proposed use and how the designer would have to detail shaft walls and structural enclosures. Adjacent occupancy groups would affect what rating the designer felt would be needed between the client's space and the existing spaces.

Knowing whether or not a building is fully sprinklered would affect maximum allowable area, finishes, and other design and detailing decisions. Fire-zone classifications are generally irrelevant for interior design work. Accessibility requirements are necessary, but the requirements themselves do not relate to the building.

44. *The answer is C.*   To determine the maximum travel distance (described in Sol. 54) allowed by the *International Building Code* (IBC), the designer must know the occupancy classification and whether or not the building is sprinklered. Travel distance is part of the exit access (described in Sol. 52) and is usually not protected. Therefore, the IBC limits the distance occupants must cross to safely exit. The maximum allowable distance is greater in sprinklered buildings than in unsprinklered buildings.

45. *The answer is A, C, and F.*   Corridors are part of the exit access portion of the egress system, not the exit portion. This means that they are used for calculating travel distance, but they do not necessarily have to be fire rated (although they usually are). Also, by definition, they must be used exclusively for egress. Dead-end corridors are allowed within certain limitations; for example, to 20 ft (6096 mm) in a nonsprinklered building.

46. *The answer is A.* The combination of a 36 in (914 mm) and a 42 in (1067 mm) door provides a total of 72 in (1829 mm) (33 in + 39 in = 72 in) of clear width. These are the minimum door widths that will satisfy the 71 in (1804 mm) total egress width requirement.

The required width for both egress doors and doors used for accessibility is the clear width, not the size of the door. Accessibility guidelines require a 32 in (813 mm) minimum clear width. The thickness of the door itself and the hinge space make the clear width for commercial door assemblies about 3 in (76 mm) less than the actual door width. A 36 in (914 mm) door has an actual clear opening of 33 in (838 mm). Therefore, a 34 in (864 mm) door (option B) cannot be used because the clear opening (about 31 in [787 mm]) would not be wide enough to comply with the accessibility requirements. The combination of a 36 in (914 mm) door and a 44 in (1118 mm) door (option C) would provide 74 in (1880 mm) of clear width (33 in + 41 in = 74 in), which would satisfy egress width requirements, but the problem statement asks for the minimum possible sizes. The combination of two 36 in (914 mm) doors (option D) would only provide 66 in (1676 mm) of clear width (33 in + 33 in = 66 in).

47. *The answer is C.* The *International Building Code* (IBC) and accessibility requirements state that handrails must be 34 in to 38 in (864 mm to 965 mm) high, as measured from the nosing. Moving the handrail down 3½ in (89 mm) and locating its top at the 36 in (915 mm) position places it within the required limits and allows the contractor some tolerance in repositioning it. Moving it up by ½ in (13 mm) to 40 in (1016 mm) (option A) would make the handrail too high. Although moving the handrail down 1½ in (38 mm) (option B) would technically place the handrail in an acceptable position, the top of the handrail would be at the upper limit of the allowable measurements, and this placement would not allow for any misalignment or tolerance. Moving it down 6 in (152 mm) to 33½ in (851 mm) (option D) would make it too low.

48. *The answer is D.* The most restrictive building type is Type I, while the least restrictive is Type IV.

49. *The answer is A.* Only tempered and laminated glass are considered to be safety glazing because they meet the requirements of 16 CFR 1201. Although the 2012 edition of the *International Building Code* (IBC) does permit the use of wired glass that meets the requirements of ANSI Z97.1 in certain applications, the question does not specify this compliance. Furthermore, neither wired glass nor heat-strengthened glass meet the requirements of 16 CFR 1201.

50. *The answer is C.* The only way to locate sprinklers such that the maximum spacing between heads is 15 ft (4570 mm) and the maximum spacing from the walls is 7½ ft (2285 mm) is to use four heads.

51. *The answer is D.* The occupancy and occupant load are used to determine the number of exits.

52. *The answer is C.* There are three parts to a building's means of egress, or exit path, which go from the least protected to the most protected. The *exit access* (e.g., room, aisle, hallway, or ramp) leads to the exit. Depending on occupancy and construction type, the exit access may or may not be protected.

The *exit* (e.g., exterior exit door, exit enclosure for stairs, or exit passageway) provides a protected path of egress between the exit access and the exit discharge. It must always be protected by fire-resistance-rated construction.

The *exit discharge* (e.g., exterior exit stairway, exit court, or exterior exit balcony) is the portion of the egress system between the termination of the exit and a public way. The discharge must be unobstructed, sprinklered, and clearly visible from the exit termination point.

53. *The answer is A.* Exits must always be protected by fire-resistance-rated construction. They are not limited in length. Exits may be as simple as exterior exit doors at ground level or may include exit enclosures for stairways. Depending on the building height, construction type, and passageway length, exits must have either a 1- or 2-hour rating.

54. *The answer is B.* The two main factors used to determine whether a space needs more than one exit are the occupancy and the occupant load. The *occupancy* is how the space is used (e.g., business, industrial, or residential). The *occupant load* is the maximum number of people that may occupy the space. If the occupant load exceeds the allowable value given in the *International Building Code* (IBC), then one or more additional exits will be needed.

Though the occupant load and occupancy are the most important factors in determining how many exits a space must have, a third factor—the travel distance—is also considered. The *travel distance* is the measurable distance from a space's most remote occupiable point to the entrance of the nearest exit that serves it. If this distance exceeds the limits given in the IBC, a second exit will be required, even if the occupant load is within the allowable value given in the IBC.

Exit width, however, is not a factor in determining a space's required number of exits.

55. *The answer is C.* The solution that is least expensive and most sensitive to accessibility requirements is to provide a power-assisted door opener.

56. *The answer is C.* All the sink installations listed as possible options can work if they meet the measurement requirements shown in the following illustration, but a wall-hung lavatory gives the most open access, usually exceeding the minimum requirements.

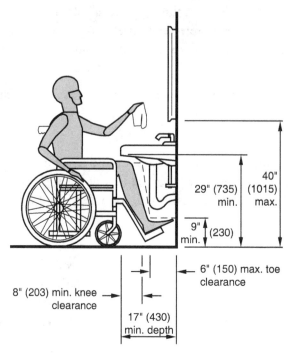

lavatory clearances

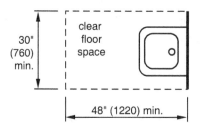

clear floor space at lavatories

57. *The answer is D.* Wood wall finishes of paneling or wainscoting are regulated in the same way as other wall and ceiling finishes. The minimum flame-spread rating depends on the occupancy and the location in the building.

58. *The answer is C.* For light hazard occupancies, NFPA 13 requires one sprinkler for each 225 ft² (18.6 m²) of area. This means a maximum spacing of 15 ft (4572 mm) is permitted between sprinklers. In addition, no sprinkler can be farther than 7½ ft (2286 mm) from any wall.

59. *The answer is C.* The standard tile in a 2 ft × 2 ft (610 mm × 610 mm) standard T-bar grid provides a similar aesthetic and reduces the cost enough to conform to the construction budget (15,000 ft² × $0.60 savings/ft² = $9000 savings).

The cost for each system needs to be calculated to determine which alternative will reduce the price of the system by at least $6000. However, first the interior designer needs to identify which system(s) will meet the owner's requirement of maintaining the specified acoustical performance and will provide a similar aesthetic. The drywall alternate clearly differs from the grid aesthetic and would not provide the sound-absorbing qualities of an acoustical tile ceiling, so this is an inappropriate choice. The 2 ft × 4 ft (610 mm × 1220 mm) grid system would save the most money, but does not provide the same aesthetic as a 2 ft × 2 ft (610 mm × 610 mm) grid. The 2 ft × 2 ft (610 mm × 610 mm) narrow grid ceiling would comply with the acoustical performance requirements, but would only save $3000 (15,000 ft² × $0.20 savings/ ft² = $3000 savings)

60. *The answer is A.*   The best source for independent, third-party information specifically about a carpet's VOC emissions is the Carpet and Rug Institute's Green Label Plus program. This program tests carpets (as well as cushions and adhesives) to identify products that have low VOC emissions.

While the *GreenSpec Directory* (which is a directory of environmentally preferable products) and the Greenguard Environmental Institute (which establishes indoor air standards for indoor products) will have information about a carpet's VOCs, neither of these is specific to carpet. The U.S. Green Building Council developed the LEED rating systems; it does not produce information about carpet VOC emissions.

61. *The answer is A.*   Of the possible choices, option A is the most correct because it implies that the amount of fuel would be reduced, regardless of the fabric material, whether or not it was fire-retardant treated, or what type of weave it had.

62. *The answer is A.*   Seismic design categories D, E, and F are the most restrictive and require that ceiling-high partitions be braced independently from the ceiling grid. Option B is incorrect because the IBC states that the seismic design category must be determined by a structural engineer or architect, not by the interior designer. Option C is incorrect because in seismic design categories D, E, and F, the ceiling grid must be attached to the ceiling angles on two adjacent walls and not attached on the opposite sides of those walls to allow for movement. In seismic design category C, the grid must not be attached to any of the perimeter trim. Option D is incorrect because compression struts and lateral bracing are required at 12 ft, or 144 in (3.66 m), on center.

❺ INTERIOR BUILDING MATERIALS AND FINISHES

63. *The answer is C.*   All carpet manufactured or sold in the United States is required to pass the methenamine pill test. The flooring radiant panel test is used for corridor flooring and types of flooring in only a few occupancies. The Steiner tunnel test can be used, but it is not a realistic test on carpet because the material is tested on top of the tunnel.

64. *The answer is B, C, D, and F.* Barrier-free design requires that objects not protrude into the accessible path in such a way as to present a hazard. In addition, tactile signs must have a minimum $^1/_{32}$ in (0.79 mm) raised surface, and accessible routes must not be reduced in width. Room identification signs must be in uppercase. The color is not critical as long as there is contrast between the lettering and the background. Fonts must be san serif or simple serif, but there is no standard ADA font. Refer to the following illustration.

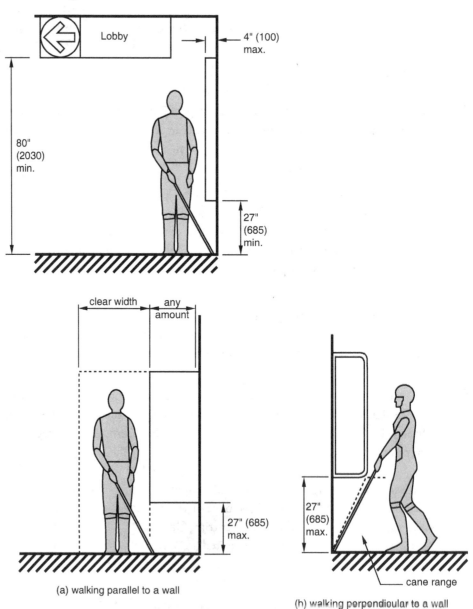

(a) walking parallel to a wall

(h) walking perpendicular to a wall

65. *The answer is D.* Plenum access precludes the use of gypsum wallboard for the ceiling unless many access panels were used, which is costly and can become unsightly with use. Both integrated ceilings and linear metal strip ceilings provide for some access, but their cost in a large commercial project would not be warranted. An integrated ceiling may be a good choice, but the question does not give enough information about the parameters of the problem to make this a reasonable option.

66. *The answer is C.* Although the sheet material indicated in the drawing may help minimize squeaking, the fact that a wood floor is shown over a concrete floor should indicate that the material shown is a vapor barrier.

67. *The answer is A.* Because slate does not have a uniform thickness and a concrete subfloor above grade may deflect and cause cracking, the best installation is a thick-set method with a cleavage membrane. The thick-set method allows the tile setter to adjust the bed according to the exact thickness of each stone, and a cleavage membrane (with reinforcement) allows the finish floor to float above any slight deflection of the concrete floor.

68. *The answer is B.* Pitch is the number of ends of surface yarn in a 27 in (686 mm) width. To convert this measurement to gauge (the spacing between stitches), divide 27 in (686 mm) into 216 stitches. This gives 8 stitches/in, or 8 surface yarns/in. The equivalent gauge, therefore, is 1/8.

69. *The answer is C.* Integrated ceiling systems are proprietary suspended systems designed to accommodate ceiling tile, lights, supply air devices, return air grilles, sprinklers, and other ceiling-mounted elements, as well as partition attachment. Such a system can easily provide for frequent changes in room configuration with accompanying changes in lighting and HVAC layout.

Designing and manufacturing a custom track system would be very expensive and unnecessary for one job, as there are other available products. A 60 in (1524 mm) lay-in acoustical grid would only work with a demountable partitions system, and while such a system provides for changes, it is more expensive that an integrated ceiling system, which also provides for easy changes to mechanical and electrical components. A narrow bar exposed T-bar system is simply a type of grid system and does not make changes easier.

70. *The answer is A.* By definition, curtains are generally not intended to be opened.

71. *The answer is D.* Although the cleaning agent manufacturer would provide warnings about the health effects of its products, the most unbiased source is the *safety data sheet.* The flooring manufacturer would only list the recommended cleaning agents and not be responsible for detailing potential hazards of the cleaning agent itself. The EPA does not have information about individual cleaning products; it would only have information about the base chemicals that would be constituent parts.

72. *The answer is C.* Of the options listed, vinyl wallcovering offers the best balance of low cost and durability. Either a Type II or Type III wallcovering could be selected based on the project budget and the amount of durability required. Depending on the type of material selected, fabric wallcovering can be expensive and will not provide protection from people and furniture rubbing against it. Thin stone tiles are durable but are more expensive per square foot than vinyl wallcovering. Wood veneer paneling can be a durable wall treatment but costs more than vinyl.

73. *The answer is C.* Every manufacturer knows the limitations of its products and should be consulted when one of its products is going to be used in a specific, special situation that the interior designer knows about. Although the other three sources may be consulted for additional information, only the manufacturer knows the limitations of a product.

74. *The answer is B.* Sheet vinyl minimizes the number of joints and is resistant to grease, oils, and water.

75. *The answer is C.* The device shown is a proprietary acoustic clip, which is used to provide resiliency of the gypsum wallboard mounted to it, thereby reducing the transmission of vibrations (sound) through the partition. In order to minimize reverberation or increase the SAA (which is also known as the noise reduction coefficient [NRC]), some type of absorptive material would be required instead of the hard-surface gypsum wallboard shown, so options A and B are incorrect. Although this construction assembly could decrease impact noise (option D), such noise transmission is commonly related to floor-ceiling construction rather than partition wall assemblies, and is not the primary purpose of using this type of clip.

❻ TECHNICAL SPECIFICATIONS FOR FURNITURE, FIXTURES, & EQUIPMENT AND LIGHTING

76. *The answer is B.* In a fabric showroom, accurate color rendition is an important concern. Therefore, options B and D are the most likely choices. Although the color temperature rating of a lamp gives a general indication of the lamp's "whiteness," the color rendering index (or "CRI") is a more accurate indication of how appropriate a lamp is for a specific application.

77. *The answer is D.* A grazing light from a point source close to the wall would best emphasize the wall's texture. The other types of lighting would appear to flatten the wall's surface.

78. *The answer is B.* Quarter slicing results in the straightest grain possible from most species of trees, as shown in the following illustration.

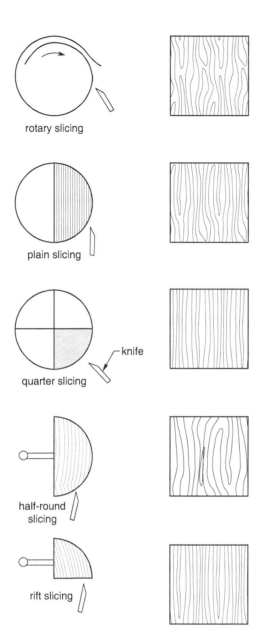

rotary slicing

plain slicing

quarter slicing

knife

half-round slicing

rift slicing

79. *The answer is B.*   Of the options listed, only book matching and slip matching refer to the ways individual veneer pieces can be laid up next to each other. Of these two options, book matching is generally considered the preferred, most pleasing method. Balance matching and center matching refer to methods of applying veneers to panels.

80. *The answer is D.*   Wool is the most fire-resistant natural fiber. Cotton is the most flammable unless it is treated.

81. *The answer is B.*   Theater seating requires a fabric that is resilient, durable, and flame retardant. The only combination that meets these requirements is the wool-nylon blend.

82. *The answer is D.* Because there are so many variables that affect the interaction of light sources and the objects they are illuminating, the *best* way to evaluate a specific situation is to look at samples of the specified materials and finishes under the specific light sources under consideration. There are typically several different colors of finishes and furniture fabrics in any given space, and while one type of lamp may render one color perfectly, it may shift the apparent color of another. Only by observing all the object colors under different lamps can the interior designer select the one that provides the best overall balance.

Option A is incorrect because the CRI is only a measure of how well one light source renders color compared to a reference source. While generally speaking, the higher the CRI the better, two light sources can have the same CRI but entirely different chromaticities, and therefore render the same color differently. Option B would be the second-best way to evaluate lamps because the CCT would suggest whether the light source would enhance or dull the object color. For example, a lamp with a low color temperature and more blue components, like a cool-white fluorescent lamp, would render reds dull and washed out. As the question asks for the best way to select the lamps, option B is incorrect. Option C is incorrect because the spectral energy distribution curves would show only what colors predominate, and, like using the CCT, would give only an approximation of adequate color rendering.

83. *The answer is A, B, D, and F.* A lighting cove is a form of indirect lighting that is built into recesses or ceiling valences and may be used as primary lighting or for aesthetic accent. Cost, design intent, aesthetics, and lighting levels are all important criteria an interior designer should consider when designing a lighting cove. However, it is not important to consider ergonomics for a design element that occupants do not physically use or come in direct contact with. Although the framing method would have to be detailed, this is not as important, as there are many ways to detail lighting coves.

84. *The answer is B.* The three most important characteristics to assess in a custom-blended fabric that will be used in a public area are its wearability, flammability, and fade-resistivity. While any fabric can be treated to make it flame resistive, only testing can determine whether a custom fabric has sufficient wearability and fade-resistance for a specific use. The Wyzenbeek abrasion resistance test is commonly used to assess wearability, while the Fade-Ometer test is used to assess fade-resistance.

A vertical ignition test is used with textiles and films, and an indentation load deflection test is used with cushioning, not fabric. The Wyzenbeek and Taber tests both assess wearability, so both would not be specified.

85. *The answer is C.* NFPA 701, *Standard Methods of Fire Tests for Flame-Propagation of Textiles and Films*, establishes testing procedures for window treatments. This is also known as FR 701, so the important thing is to recognize the 701 designation.

86. *The answer is B.* Building codes generally require flame-spread classification for wall finishes only; this includes wainscoting. Other types of woodwork, such as bookshelves, cabinets, and door and window trim, do not require a particular fire rating.

87. *The answer is 30 fc.* For a point source of light, the illumination, E, on a surface varies directly with the luminous intensity, I, of the source and inversely with the square of the distance, d, between the source and the point.

The formula for illumination is

$$E = \frac{I}{d^2}$$
$$= \frac{1470}{7^2}$$
$$= 30 \text{ fc}$$

88. *The answer is D.* Channeling is a method of attaching fabric to a cushion and direct attachment is the best way to avoid slippage. Therefore, option D is the best choice.

89. *The answer is D.* The furniture plan typically contains only a code number for each piece of furniture. This code number refers either to a schedule on the drawings or to the specifications, where detailed information is listed, such as the furniture's manufacturer, model number, color, finish, and so on.

90. *The answer is C.* The slip resistance of flooring is measured using the DCOF AcuTest. This is the designated test procedure of the Tile Council of North America. It measures the dynamic coefficient of friction (DCOF) using a standard lubricant on ceramic tile. Other materials may respond differently.

Variables that can affect safety include shoe material and the degree of its wear, the presence and nature of surface contaminants, a person's weight, the angle of impact, stride length, the wear of the flooring material, and whether the floor is flat or inclined. All these factors should be taken into account when specifying a flooring material.

The DCOF value of 0.42 is the recommended minimum value for ceramic tile as contained in American National Standards Institute (ANSI) Standard A137.1, *Specifications for Ceramic Tile*. While this is a good starting point, the designer should consider other variables that can affect the safety of the floor.

Simply specifying a rough finish may not be enough, as the definition of "rough" is ambiguous. The test in ASTM Standard C1082 is no longer used and has been withdrawn.

91. *The answer is B.* The COF is used to evaluate and specify flooring materials. This value expresses the degree of slip resistance of a flooring material. Although there are many variables that affect the slip resistance of a flooring material, and no one value is universally agreed upon for all situations, the COF is the one value that must be known. Currently, in the United States, American National Standards Institute (ANSI) standard A137.1, *American National Standards Specifications for Ceramic Tile*, references one test, the DCOF AcuTest (DCOF stands for *dynamic coefficient of friction*). This requires that ceramic tile for level interior spaces expected to be walked upon when wet must have a minimum value equal to or greater than 0.42. However, this is just a starting point; the interior designer should consider the type of flooring material being evaluated, specific conditions of the space in which it will be used, expected maintenance procedures, and other project-specific variables to determine if a material with a higher COF should be specified.

Option A is incorrect because it is likely the material will already have been tested to determine the COF. Option C is incorrect because current ADA and ABA (Architectural Barriers Act) requirements call for a slip-resistant surface for flooring without giving a specific value for the COF. Option D is incorrect because the ASTM International standards that still exist for slip resistance have been replaced with the ANSI A137.1 standard.

92. *The answer is B.* Of the four plans given, only the reflected ceiling plan would normally show exit signs. Exit signs are shown on this plan so that their positions can be coordinated with those of other items on the ceiling. Exit signs are also shown on the electrical engineer's lighting plan, which indicates how they are powered and circuited to the emergency circuits.

93. *The answer is A.* The coefficient of utilization (commonly abbreviated "CU") is a value that is determined and published by the manufacturer. It represents the efficiency of a luminaire in distributing light from a lamp under various degrees of finish reflectivity to the floor, walls, and ceiling.

94. *The answer is B.* Although all the choices are possible reasons for using surface-mounted luminaires, the lighting fixtures are most often employed when space is inadequate for recessing.

❼ CONSTRUCTION DRAWINGS, SCHEDULES, AND SPECIFICATIONS

95. *The answer is A, B, C, and E.* Cover sheets for interior design construction drawings commonly include building department data, the client's name and address, indexes to drawings, and the symbols used. Cover sheets do not contain a small-scale floor plan or zoning department information.

96. *The answer is C.* Composite wood veneer is an artificial product that uses readily available and fast-growing renewable trees to make veneers that are stained and reformed into an artificial log that is then sliced to produce new veneer. It is considered a sustainable or "green" product.

97. *The answer is A, C, E, and F.* The finish schedule or plan, means of egress, mechanical drawings, and interior space plan (among other items) are all required by the IBC to be submitted for review. Architectural millwork details and custom furniture drawings are seldom required.

98. *The answer is C.* A scribe piece is ideal in this case because it can be trimmed in the field so the edge of a cabinet or countertop can exactly fit the irregularities of the wall, which are common when working with existing construction. A reveal can only be useful in this case if the designer specifies that the piece can be scribed to fit. Otherwise, it is a recessed piece that will likely be perfectly straight and therefore may result in gaps between the cabinet and the irregular wall.

Blocking and spacers are not directly related to fit and appearance of cabinets next to existing construction. Cabinets are constructed so only the frames and edges touch existing construction; the backs of cabinets are constructed to stand out from the wall by a small amount. A spacer is a small, thin piece of wood placed between the back of the cabinet and the wall at fastener locations to prevent the cabinet back from bowing outward when a fastener is used to attach the cabinet to the wall. Blocking is used inside a wall to provide a solid piece of construction to which the cabinet can be fastened.

99. *The answer is C.* Polyurethane and polyester are both very durable, synthetic finishes.

100. *The answer is A, D, E and F.* Furniture plans for commercial projects must always include partitions and the location and code number of all furniture items to distinguish specific items. Telephone, data, and power outlet locations are sometimes shown to relate the furniture with required services. Desk lamp locations and computers are not shown because they are plugged into power outlets already shown.

101. *The answer is A.* The methods in options B and C are useful in writing concise specifications but are not as good as using industry standards, which eliminate a great deal of text. Option D is incorrect because a descriptive specification requires lengthy text to fully and accurately describe what the specifier wants.

102. *The answer is B.* The drawing shows the locations of power outlets and lines, and notes indicating to which circuit each outlet is connected. Although it also shows telephone outlet locations, it is primarily a power plan.

The term electrical plan is too generic to be useful and is not a correct choice. A telephone/electrical plan is drawn by the interior designer to show the outlets dimensioned and in relation to furniture, and is used by the electrical engineer to produce the power plan. No lighting is shown, so this is not a lighting plan.

103. *The answer is C.* Ornamental metalwork is included in Division 05, "Metals," in the MasterFormat system. Doors are specified in Division 08, "Openings." Wall finishes are included in Division 09, "Finishes," and architectural woodwork is contained in Division 06, "Woods, Plastics, and Composites."

104. *The answer is C.* Furniture drawings are prepared during a project's contract documents phase. The consultant contracts should be coordinated early in the project— either before the project is begun or during the schematic design phase. A code review should be performed during the schematic design and design development phase. Shop drawings are reviewed during the contract administration phase.

105. *The answer is A, B, E and F.* Floor plans reference the door schedule using a symbol and a number to represent each door. The door schedule is included on the project drawings and lists specific information about each door. The specifications define the characteristics of each of the specified door types and also contain the hardware schedule. Shop drawings from the door supplier also show detailed information about the doors.

Although room elevations show doors, they do not convey important or detailed information about the doors. Enlarged floor plans are drawn for reasons other than to show door information.

106. *The answer is A, B, D and F.* Showing dimensions on only the drawings, having someone check the drawings before they are issued, ensuring that terminology used in the specifications matches that used on the drawings, and using master specifications are all actions that an interior designer may take to minimize potential conflicts in the contract documents.

The specifications should be outlined and written while the drawings are in progress, not after they are completed. The person writing the specifications and the project manager or job captain should be in constant contact while both documents are being completed to minimize conflicts. Drawing sheet organization should follow a standard format regardless of the particular job. This helps those working on the drawings to make sure the required information is included where it is required and relates to other drawings.

107. *The answer is D.* Division 12, "Furnishings," of the MasterFormat system includes window treatments, as well as furniture, accessories, and art. Division 08 is "Openings," Division 09 is "Finishes," and Division 10 is "Specialties."

108. *The answer is C.* The elevations shown are small graphical representations of the various door and frame types used on a project. They are identified by letters that would also be part of the door schedule, which refers to the elevations to give additional details about these building components.

109. *The answer is A.* The reflected ceiling plan should show slab-to-slab partitions as well as ceiling-high partitions. Although this information is usually indicated on wall-section details and sometimes on interior elevations, the reflected ceiling plan is the one place where it is all shown at once in an obvious manner.

110. *The answer is B.* For interior design drawings, partitions are commonly dimensioned to the finished face of the wall. This is because the interior designer is most concerned with finishes and any critical dimensions that may exist between one partition and another. Option A is incorrect because dimensioning to the centerlines of partitions requires that the designer be aware of each partition's thickness and calculate the dimension accordingly, which can lead to errors in the desired size of the space. Option C is sometimes used by architects for the convenience of the contractor because it simplifies stud layout. However, this approach can result in slight errors in the desired finished size of a space, especially when the finish requires installation of additional furring or thick finish materials. Option D is incorrect because structural walls are dimensioned from their finished face, not their centerline. However, dimensions are typically made to the centerline of columns.

111. *The answer is D.* High-rise building drawings commonly include the floor number as part of the sheet number so it is clear to everyone on the project team (including the building owner or manager) what floor the plan and other drawings refer to. The sheet number also indicates who created the drawings: interior designer (A), structural engineer (S), mechanical engineer (M), electrical engineer (E), and so on. The correct notation indicates that the drawings were created by the interior designer and are referring to the 23rd floor.

112. *The answer is B, D, E, and F.* On a small-scale plan, there is not enough room to include dimensions to fixtures, all the required wall dimensions, toilet partition dimensions, and keynotes for accessories, so these would be shown on the large-scale plan. Option A is incorrect because the room names and numbers are also shown on the small-scale plan. Option C is incorrect because the toilet partition door swings should also be shown on the small-scale plan.

113. *The answer is C.* On a demolition plan, dashed lines most commonly represent materials being removed and solid lines (or solid black fill) represent materials being reused.

114. *The answer is B.* Fastener spacing for wallboard and other panel products should either be listed or referenced as an industry standard in the project's specifications. Edge treatments, stud depths, and wallboard thicknesses are always part of a project's drawings.

115. *The answer is A, C, D, and E.*   Because windows are part of the architectural work in a building, a window schedule would not be found in a set of interior design drawings. Information on specific types of toilet accessories to be provided would be included in the specifications, not on the drawings.

116. *The answer is D.*   The drawing is a reflected ceiling plan because it includes symbols for lighting, supply air diffusers, and elevations above the floor. If it were a lighting plan, there would be no elevation symbols.

It is not a floor plan because it does not include elements such as door openings, dimensions, or elevation symbols. It is not a finish plan because it does not include typical finish plan symbology such as rectangles with numbers and letters, or lines running from corners to corners with attached notes.

117. *The answer is A.*   Demolition plans are typically included in the drawing set when the complexity of the project is such that trying to place all the information about elements to be removed and new work to be constructed on the construction floor plan would be too confusing. With a demolition plan, all the dimensions, notes, reference symbols, and other information normally found on a floor plan can be omitted, leaving just the items to be removed indicated with dashed lines, and existing construction to remain indicated with solid lines. Additional notes can be included indicating what items are to be reused or recycled, if necessary.

Option B is incorrect because AHJs do not require demolition plans by themselves, only enough information to show the AHJ what is being removed and what is new construction, which can be shown on the construction plan. Option C is incorrect because a sustainability plan does not require a demolition plan for recycling or reuse, although it is a convenient way to convey this information. Option D is incorrect because contractors do not request the types of drawings produced by the interior designer.

118. *The answer is B.*   The detail shown is a slip joint where a partition attaches to the vertical window mullion. The aluminum channel is attached to the window mullion while the partition is constructed separately, allowing the curtain wall to move in and out with wind loading without putting any pressure on the partition.

Option A is incorrect because the detail is not of a modular partition. Option C is incorrect because the end of the partition could be finished with gypsum wallboard casing beads. Option D is incorrect because this detail actually is a weak point for blocking sound transmission.

119. *The answer is C.*   In the following illustration, any portion of a drawing falling within the circle or the dashed rounded rectangle will be shown in the same view (plan view, for example) at an enlarged scale with more detail shown.

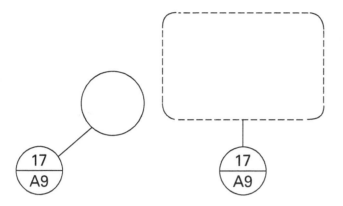

❽ PROFESSIONAL DEVELOPMENT AND ETHICS

120. *The answer is B.* According to the American Society of Interior Designers (ASID) Code of Ethics, in the section Responsibility to the Client, the designer must fully disclose to the client all compensation the designer will receive in connection with a project.

The interior designer is allowed to offer services for any form of legal compensation. Having a financial interest in the project may not provide the designer with direct compensation, but it may affect the designer's judgment concerning how the project may be designed.

An employee is allowed to take drawings, data, and other material, but only with the permission of the employer.

According to the section Responsibility to the Profession, designers agree to encourage and contribute to the sharing of ideas and information. For example, it is acceptable for a designer to share his or her experience and knowledge of a particular project type with another designer who is working on a similar project.

121. *The answer is A.* The American Society of Interior Design (ASID) Code of Ethics requires that the interior designer consider the health, safety, and welfare of the public at all times. The designer should tell the client that the designer cannot use the chairs, and show the client the information to support this decision. Only then should the designer look for substitutes.

The designer should not give the task of finding alternative chairs to the client. The client will not be aware of the safety requirements. To accept the chairs while disregarding the safety issues would be a clear violation of the Code of Ethics section Responsibility to the Client. Before the designer looks for substitute chairs that meet Business and International Furniture Manufacturers Association (BIFMA) standards, the designer should first explain to the client why the designer is taking this action.

122. *The answer is C.* The American Society of Interior Designers (ASID) Code of Ethics has a section titled Responsibility to the Employer that the International Interior Design Association (IIDA) Code of Ethics does not. This section outlines the ethical relationship between the employer and the employee. For example, a designer (as an employee) cannot disclose any confidential information obtained during the course of his or her employment without the permission of both the client and the employer.

123. *The answer is D.* Teaching is an excellent way for interior designers to share their knowledge as well as gaining knowledge. Teaching also helps in the development of students and professionals and in serving the community. The other options listed can be valuable ways to get involved outside of the office, but teaching offers all three possibilities.

124. *The answer is D.* American Society of Interior Designers (ASID) is organized to serve its members (constituency-based), engage in political advocacy such as licensing (cause-based), and provide continuing education with seminars, conventions, and other activities (knowledge-based).

125. *The answer is A, B, D, and E.* Continuing education is most importantly needed so that designers can keep up to date with constant changes in technology, building materials and methods, legal requirements, and practice procedures. Continuing education is also useful as a way to advance a designer's career, to maintain membership in professional organizations such as the American Society of Interior Designers (ASID) and the International Interior Design Association (IIDA), and to maintain the same level of knowledge and competence as fellow professionals.

Continuing education is not required by all states or Canadian provinces, only those that have a practice or title that requires it. Professional organizations are motivated by reasons other than the advantages of continuing education.